East Asia Economic and Financial Out'
Gerrit W. Gong and Erik R. Peterson,

China's Domestic Economy in Regional Context

Ding Jingping

THE CENTER FOR STRATEGIC & INTERNATIONAL STUDIES
Washington, D.C.

Cover design by Hasten Design Studio.

Significant Issues Series, Volume XVII, Number 4
© 1995 by The Center for Strategic and International Studies
Washington, D.C. 20006
Printed on recycled paper in the United States of America

99   98   97   96   95   5   4   3   2   1

ISSN 0736-7136
ISBN 0-89206-318-1

Library of Congress Cataloging-in-Publication Data

Ting, Ching-p'ing, 1949–
    China's domestic economy in regional context / by Ding
Jingping ; foreword by Gerrit W. Gong and Erik R. Peterson.
        p. cm. — (Significant issues series, ISSN 0736-7136
; v. 17, no. 4.   East Asia economic and financial outlook)
Includes bibliographical references.
ISBN 0-89206-318-1
    1. China—Economic policy—1976 –   2. Economic forecasting—
China.   I. Title.   II. Series: Significant issues series ; v.
17, no. 4.   III. Series: Significant issues series.   East Asia
economic and financial outlook.
HC427.92.T56   1995
338.951—dc20   95-2138
                                                                    CIP

China's Domestic Economy in Regional Context

Significant Issues Series

SIGNIFICANT ISSUES SERIES papers are written for and published by the Center for Strategic and International Studies.

Series Editors:	David M. Abshire
	Douglas M. Johnston
Director of Studies:	Erik R. Peterson
Director of Publications:	Nancy B. Eddy
Managing Editor:	Roberta L. Howard
Associate Editor:	Donna R. Spitler
Editorial Assistant:	Kathleen M. McTigue

❖　❖　❖

The Center for Strategic and International Studies (CSIS), founded in 1962, is an independent, tax-exempt, public policy research institution based in Washington, D.C. The mission of the Center is to advance the understanding of emerging world issues in the areas of international economics, politics, security, and business. It does so by providing a strategic perspective to decision makers that is integrative in nature, international in scope, anticipatory in its timing, and bipartisan in its approach. The Center's commitment is to serve the common interests and values of the United States and other countries around the world that support representative government and the rule of law.

CSIS, as a public policy research institution, does not take specific policy positions. Accordingly, all views, positions, and conclusions expressed in this publication should be understood to be solely those of the author.

The Center for Strategic and International Studies
1800 K Street, N.W.
Washington, D.C.　20006
Telephone: (202) 887-0200
Fax: (202) 775-3199

Contents

East Asia Economic and Financial Outlook: Introduction to the Series

No doubt when future historians survey the topography of the late twentieth century, they will focus on the burst of economic activity that took place in East Asia. They will have good reason.

In a short time, many East Asian players have transformed their economic and financial systems into modern, dynamic structures generating high levels of growth and prosperity. They have propelled Asia as a region into real gross-domestic-product growth levels at or above 6.5 percent for the past two decades. They have transformed the region into one of the most competitive targets for foreign capital inflows. And they are now poised to carry forward this momentum into the third millennium.

These advances, as impressive as they are when expressed in macroeconomic terms, are all the more significant when translated into everyday life. Economic landscapes are changing fundamentally, and so too are the welfares of the populations. The new prosperity in the region is changing social patterns, generating new attitudes, and creating higher expectations. Furthermore, the change in economic and financial linkages between the East Asian economies—together with the expanded linkages between their populations—has been equally significant.

It should be stressed that this explosion of economic activity in East Asia is not the byproduct of a single driving factor such as the increase in world oil prices in the 1970s and its effect on oil-exporting states. Instead, it is being achieved through a variety of policy reorientations undertaken in significantly different economic and political structures with equally different factor endowments.

As a result, the constellation of economic, financial, political, and social changes that have culminated in the "East Asian miracle" is highly complex. While the region shares the common denominator of comparatively high levels of growth and export-driven expansion, the differences among its economies and political systems are profound. Each has its own staging point—and its own perceptions about the role its economy will play in the next century.

In thinking about the economic and financial dynamics of East Asia and the position the region is assuming in the world economy, we wanted to explore an array of economy-specific perceptions guiding policymakers in the region. A central question arises: To what extent do the plans that policymakers have for positioning their economies for the next century coincide, and to what extent do they collide?

This is the rationale for the *East Asia Economic and Financial Outlook* series published by the Asian Studies Program of the Center for Strategic and International Studies (CSIS). The series will present the insights of prominent East Asian analysts and draw conclusions about complementarities or divergences that may exist. Those insights, in turn, will serve in the aggregate as the basis for a richer, cross-cutting assessment of how the region will continue to develop and the role it can be expected to play in the quickly changing global economic and financial system.

At issue is the matrix of economy-specific considerations that characterize the region. What are the respective development strategies? Are they grounded in regionalism or globalism? How will those strategies be achieved? What additional reforms of the economic and financial systems are necessary? What comparative advantages are the economies seeking to establish as they move into the next century? These are a few of the key questions we have asked each author to address.

We begin the series with three separate analyses of "greater China," representing perspectives from Taiwan, Hong Kong, and the People's Republic of China. Such analysis must, by definition, be central to a broader regional assessment owing to the size of—and growth in—what has been referred to as the "Chinese economic area." Moreover, the ongoing political and economic redefinition of China—including the issues of succession and economic reform in Beijing, the realignment of political and economic forces in Taiwan, and the reversion of Hong Kong on July 1, 1997—suggests the importance of beginning our regional appraisal from these perspectives.

The series will include assessments of other key East Asian economies as well. With each volume, we hope to build a clearer picture of the regional contours and forces in the region that are shaping the twenty-first century economy in East Asia.

This series reflects the research and focus at CSIS on changes in the international economic and financial system. The Center has launched a number of initiatives covering a gamut of international financial issues, starting at home with an assessment of the U.S. regulatory system governing capital markets. Under the guidance of William A. Schreyer, chairman of the CSIS Board of Trustees' Executive Committee and chairman emeritus of Merrill Lynch & Company, Inc., CSIS has also been tracking global financial contingencies involving individual countries, regions, and transnational issues. Moreover, under the auspices of Maurice R. Greenberg, vice chairman of the CSIS Board of Trustees and chairman of the American International Group, Inc., CSIS is establishing a high-level international finance group that will convene regularly in New York.

We wish to thank several individuals who are contributing to this series. First, we express our deep appreciation to the authors for their analyses. Second, we acknowledge Keith W. Eirinberg, Chi J. Leng, Mary Marik, and Karen Wong of the CSIS Asian Studies Program; their commitment to this project reflects their competence and dedication. Finally, our appreciation goes to Nancy B. Eddy and Roberta L. Howard of the CSIS Publications Office for their important contributions to the production of these monographs.

GERRIT W. GONG
Freeman Chair in China Studies and
Director of Asian Studies, CSIS

ERIK R. PETERSON
Vice President and Director of Studies, CSIS
April 1995

About the Author

Ding Jinping is senior research fellow and deputy director of the Foreign Affairs Bureau of the Chinese Academy of Social Sciences (CASS) in Beijing. Dr. Ding received his Ph.D. and M.A. degrees in economics from the Department of Industrial Economics at CASS, where he served as the department's deputy director and senior research fellow and as editor of the journal *China Industrial Economics Research*. He has also been an assistant professor at the Hubei Financial and Economic College in Wuhan, Hubei Province.

Dr. Ding's international work includes the project on China and Southeast Asia at the Pacific Forum CSIS in Honolulu in 1992 and projects on China's technological imports (1988–1989) and China's industrial technological progress (1991) at the Fletcher School of Law and Diplomacy, Tufts University, Boston. Dr. Ding has also been a visiting scholar at the Alfred P. Sloan School of Management at the Massachusetts Institute of Technology.

Recent publications include *China: Accelerating Economic Growth Rate and Its Implications for the Asia-Pacific Region, Industrial Organization and Government Policies, Industrial Organization Policies*, and "Technical Transformation and Renovation in PRC Industry."

Foreword

The remarkable dynamism that has characterized East Asia over recent years has transformed not only the economic and financial contours of the region but also the topography of the global economic and financial system. The changes have been so profound that future historians may regard the "quiet revolution" that has taken place in East Asia as one of the seminal events of our times.

A number of analysts have looked closely at the reasons for the economic boom in East Asia. But what is all too often overshadowed in those assessments is the degree to which the economic players in the region share a common vision of the future.

The *East Asia Economic and Financial Outlook* series of studies addresses that critical issue. By offering differing perceptions by prominent authors on the outlook for East Asia, the series provides a new and important level of analysis. It will be useful to anyone committed to understanding how the region will develop through the end of the century and beyond.

WILLIAM A. SCHREYER
Chairman Emeritus, Merrill Lynch & Company, Inc., and
Chairman, Executive Committee, CSIS Board of Trustees

1

Introduction

The high rate of economic growth in the People's Republic of China (PRC) dates from the middle of the 1980s. In the late 1970s, China relinquished its old political theory of class struggle and turned to economic development. Its first step was to restructure industries and increase production of consumer products to meet the needs of the people. This new strategy and new industrial structure soon lifted China into an economic takeoff. In 1984, the growth rate of the gross national product (GNP) hit 14.7 percent, its highest point. During the 1980s, China's GNP grew at an average annual rate of 9.8 percent.[1]

In 1989, rampant inflation brought political turmoil that interrupted China's rapid growth. From 1989 to 1991, China's economy grew slowly. During 1989, 1990, and 1991, economic restructuring and consolidation caused China's rate of GNP growth to fall to 5.6 percent. In the meantime, ideological confusion brought on by the disintegration of the Warsaw Pact and the Soviet Union intensified the debate on the differences between capitalism and socialism, thereby also affecting economic development.

In a speech given in southern China in early 1992, Deng Xiaoping broke the ideological logjam by addressing issues of economic reform and the downturn in economic development. China began to reemphasize the central task of economic construction and to adopt a more flexible attitude toward ideology and economic policies. It called for addressing the economic realities of China's relations with the world rather than clinging to the theoretical debate between socialism and capitalism. Meanwhile, China increasingly adopted market means to achieve its Four Modernizations—in industry, agriculture, defense, and science and technology.[2] As a result, China entered another high growth period.

In 1992 and 1993, China had the world's fastest growing economy. Its rate of GNP growth rose from 8.2 percent in 1991 to

12.8 percent in 1992 and hit 13.4 percent in 1993. This dramatic change contrasted strikingly with the experience of the rest of the world, clearly revealing China's tremendous economic potential and demonstrating how government policies affect development.

After 15 years of openness, the PRC's economy has become tightly linked with the world economy. In 1994, China's total exports and imports equaled 45 percent of the country's GNP. Engagement with the world economy, however, has forced changes in China's domestic economic system. The domestic economy is also converting to a market system to allocate limited social and natural resources more efficiently. Consequently, in early 1994, the PRC government introduced a series of new economic policies regarding government revenue, taxation, monetary policy, capital investment, and foreign exchange to promote China's market economy.

China's high economic growth benefited from a changing world order characterized by a relatively stable regional security environment after the cold war's end; global industrial restructuring, especially in East Asia; the Japanese yen's rapid appreciation; and capital and technology transfers from the advanced countries. These conditions provided growth opportunities for many developing countries in addition to China. The fast-growing Chinese economy contributed, for example, to the Asia-Pacific region's dynamism as China absorbed substantial amounts of goods produced by other countries of the region.

What other effects does China's development have regionally, even globally? This volume examines China's economic future and its role in East Asia's development. It reviews China's current economic status and analyzes the effects thus far of China's economic reforms. A chapter is devoted to the contradictions and dilemmas accompanying economic development. Another chapter examines the positive and negative effects on state-owned enterprises of implementing reforms in finance, taxation, monetary policy, foreign exchange, and investment. The volume concludes with an overall assessment of the prospects for Chinese economic development and reform in the mid-1990s.

2

China's Economic and Financial Status

To review China's current economic and financial situation, this chapter examines three aspects of the PRC economy—development, reform, and foreign economic relations.

China's Economic Development: Statistical Data

In 1992 and 1993, China had the world's fastest growing economy. Gross domestic product (GDP) rose 13.2 percent in 1992 and shot up 13.4 percent in 1993. Between 1992 and 1993, the gross value of agricultural production increased by 4 percent, the gross value of industrial output, by 21.1 percent, and the gross value of tertiary industries, by 9.3 percent.

National income also increased rapidly. In 1993, it was 3.5 times that of 1985. The years 1992 and 1993 saw great growth in China's national income, lagging just behind its best growth year—1988 (see table 2.1).

In terms of fiscal and monetary growth, central government revenues rose 23.2 percent in 1993 over 1992. Expenditures were 21.2 percent greater in 1992, equal to 17 percent of GDP. The fiscal deficit was reduced from 23.66 billion yuan in 1992 to 20.50 billion yuan in 1993. Because revenues increased, government revenue for capital investment also increased from 164.62 billion yuan in 1992 to 197.14 billion yuan in 1993 (see table 2.2). Currency in circulation reached 586.5 billion yuan in 1993, an increase of 35.3 percent over the previous year.[3]

The real increase in average per capita income in 1993 was 10.2 percent over 1992. In 1993, the real income of each urban resident was 3,236 yuan, an increase of 19.4 percent over 1992, while that of each rural resident was 921 yuan, an increase of 17.5 percent over 1992.

Capital investment in China reached an all-time high in 1993. Real growth in social investment in fixed assets increased by 22 percent in 1993, accounting for 37.7 percent of GDP. Investment

Table 2.1
China's Economic Status, 1985–1993
(in billion yuan and in percentages)

Year	GNP	GDP	National income	Investment in fixed assets[a]	Bank credit
1985	855.76	852.74	702.0	254.32	–
	(12.8)	(12.9)	(24.2)	–	–
1986	969.63	968.76	785.9	–	759.04
	(8.1)	(8.5)	(12.0)	–	–
1987	1,130.10	1,130.71	931.3	–	903.24
	(10.9)	(11.1)	(18.5)	–	(19.0)
1988	1,406.82	1,407.42	1,173.8	449.65	1,055.13
	(11.3)	(11.3)	(26.0)	–	(16.8)
1989	1,599.33	1,599.76	1,317.6	413.77	1,240.93
	(4.4)	(4.3)	(12.2)	(-0.8)	(17.6)
1990	1,769.53	1,768.13	1,438.4	444.93	1,516.64
	(4.1)	(3.9)	(9.1)	(7.5)	(22.2)
1991	2,023.63	2,018.83	1,655.7	550.88	1,804.40
	(8.2)	(8.0)	(15.1)	(23.8)	(19.0)
1992	2,403.62	2,402.02	2,022.3	785.50	2,161.55
	(13.0)	(13.2)	(22.1)	(42.6)	(19.8)
1993	–	3,138.00	2,488.2	1,182.90	2,646.10
	–	(13.4)	(23.4)	(50.6)	(22.4)

Sources: *Statistical Yearbook of China, 1993*, pp. 31, 33, 145, and 664; *Economic Daily,* March 25, 1994, p. 2.

Note: Yuan-denominated figures are in terms of current year's prices (not adjusted for inflation); percentages are in terms of comparable, or inflation-adjusted, prices.

[a] Full social investment.

by state-owned entities, 70.3 percent of total, climbed a nominal 57.8 percent over 1992. Investment by collectives, 17.7 percent of total investment, rose 53.9 percent over 1992. Private investment, making up the remaining 12 percent of total investment, increased of 15.9 percent over the year before.

Between 1991 and 1993, total investment in fixed assets more than doubled. The share originating from state-owned enterprises rose in 1993 to 70.34 percent, up from 65.86 percent in 1991. The role of state-owned capital investment has become more important than at any time since 1985 (see table 2.3).

Table 2.2
China's Fiscal Status, 1985–1993
(in billion yuan and in percentages)

Year	Fiscal revenue	Fiscal expenditure	Balance	Revenue for investment
1985	186.64 (24.3)	184.48 (26.3)	2.16	89.50
1986	226.03 (21.1)	233.08 (26.3)	-7.05	123.47
1987	236.89 (4.8)	244.85 (5.0)	-7.96	126.00
1988	262.80 (10.9)	270.66 (10.5)	-7.86	139.70
1989	294.79 (12.2)	304.02 (12.3)	-9.23	143.53
1990	331.26 (12.4)	345.22 (13.6)	-13.96	154.62
1991	361.09 (9.0)	381.36 (10.5)	-20.27	160.86
1992	415.31 (15.0)	438.97 (15.1)	-23.66	164.62
1993	511.48	531.98	-20.50	197.14

Sources: *Statistical Yearbook of China, 1993*, pp. 215 and 221; *Economic Daily,* March 25, 1994, p. 2.

Note: Yuan-denominated figures are in terms of current year's prices (not adjusted for inflation); percentages are in terms of comparable, or inflation-adjusted, prices.

Economic Reform

The years 1992 and 1993 were productive years for China's economic reform. The two most important events were the 14th National Congress of the Chinese Communist Party (CCP) in October 1992 and the Third Plenum of the 14th National Congress of the CCP in November 1993. The October 1992 conference established a new goal: transforming China's original planned economic system into a socialist market economy. The November 1993 conference detailed plans for reaching that goal through reforms in banking and finance, taxation, capital investment, and foreign exchange to begin in early 1994.

In addressing state-owned enterprise reform, Chinese officials accelerated implementation of "The Regulations for

Table 2.3
China's Full Social Investment in Fixed Assets, 1988–1993
(in billion yuan and in percentages)

	1988	1989	1990	1991	1992	1993
Total investment	449.65	413.77	444.93	550.88	785.50	1,182.9
1. By ownership						
State-owned	276.30	253.55	291.86	362.81	527.36	832.1
Collectives	71.17	57.00	52.95	69.78	135.93	209.2
Private	102.21	103.23	100.12	118.29	122.20	141.6
2. By capital source						
State budget	41.00	34.16	38.77	37.30	33.42	–
Domestic loan	92.67	71.64	87.09	129.22	215.20	–
Foreign investment	25.90	27.42	27.83	31.63	45.71	–
Self-collected capital	290.01[a]	235.56	232.95	287.86	402.46	–
Other	–	45.01	58.30	64.88	88.70	–
Total percentage	100.00	100.00	100.00	100.00	100.00	100.00
1. By ownership						
State-owned	61.45	61.28	65.60	65.86	67.13	70.34
Collectives	15.83	13.78	11.90	12.67	17.31	17.69
Private	22.72	24.94	22.50	21.47	15.56	11.97
2. By capital source						
State budget	9.12	8.26	8.71	6.77	4.25	–
Domestic loan	20.61	17.31	19.57	23.46	27.40	–
Foreign investment	5.76	6.63	6.25	5.74	5.82	–
Self-collected capital	64.51[a]	56.93	52.36	52.25	51.24	–
Other	–	10.87	13.11	11.78	11.29	–

Source: Adapted from *Statistical Yearbook of China, 1993*, p. 145.

[a] Including other capital sources.

Shifting Operational Mechanisms for State-owned Enterprises," first announced in 1992. All central government and provincial government departments adopted additional guidelines for implementing this regulation. The stockholding system proceeded gradually: as of 1993, there were more than 130 stockholding companies in China, up from 55 in 1992.

According to the plan outlined at the Third Plenum, China in 1994 would organize and implement in all state-owned enterprises a modern enterprise system borrowed from companies in market economies. Practices in the modern enterprise system would clarify property rights relations, and Chinese state-owned enterprises could then hold operating rights and would be responsible for their own profits and losses. The goal was to increase motivation and efficiency in state-owned enterprises.

Price reforms continue: fixed prices of products and services in strongly competitive sectors of the economy are being freed to reach their market-determined level. Dual price systems for inputs of production—that is, two-tier pricing systems whereby the producer can sell goods at market prices after selling a certain quota of the product to the government—have been largely replaced by market prices for iron, steel, petroleum, electricity, coal, and other similar items.

Efforts to minimize government planning are ongoing. The state plan in 1993 covered only 5 percent of the gross value of industrial output, down from 70 percent in 1979.

In 1993, China undertook important foreign trade reforms. Since the end of 1992, the Chinese government reduced tariffs for 3,371 items—53 percent of levied items. Consequently, central government revenues decreased to 7.3 percent of the total tariff accrued. The central government also provided greater transparency in import licensing by providing lists of affected products, the departments that issue the licenses, and application and inspection procedures.

The Chinese government controls the import of only 53 products; most are important raw materials such as steel, rubber, timber, and wool, and equipment such as aircraft and automobiles. Within this group of 53 items, the central government controls only 16 items. The remainder are controlled by the provincial governments.

Foreign Economic Relations

Foreign economic relations are currently the most dynamic aspect of China's economy. According to State Bureau of

Customs statistics, total Chinese imports and exports reached
$195.72 billion in 1993, 18.2 percent greater than in 1992.
Imports were $103.95 billion, an increase of 29 percent over
1992, but exports were $91.77 billion, an increase of only 8
percent. The resulting deficit was $12.18 billion.

Primary products as a share of total exports decreased by 4.6
percent; but the share of manufacturing products increased 9
percent between 1992 and 1993. Most of the increase in exports
consisted of garments and textile products with a total export
value of $27.13 billion, an increase of 7.2 percent. This increase
was followed by machinery and electrical goods with a total
value of $22.7 billion, 16.1 percent higher than in 1992. Other
exports—shoes, toys, tourist products, plastic products, furni-
ture, and cigarettes—also saw continued increases. Most of the
export decrease was in petroleum, refined oil, coal, steel, nonfer-
rous metal, cement, and raw silk.

By the end of 1993, foreign-invested enterprises drove much
of China's export growth; these firms exported goods worth
$25.24 billion, 45.4 percent over 1992. Exports from foreign-
invested firms became a major source of hard currency for the
government. In 1993, the share of foreign-invested enterprises in
China's total external trade jumped to 34.3 percent from 20 percent in 1992 and reached a total of $67.07 billion.

Of China's export markets, Hong Kong, the United States,
Japan, and the European Union (EU) dominate. Total value of
exports to these economies in 1993 was $56.75 billion, almost
identical to 1992. But exports to the former Soviet Union and
Eastern European countries, although modest at $3.33 billion,
grew 34.8 percent over 1992.

China's imports of machinery and electric products, 47.6 percent of total imports, were worth $49.5 billion, an increase of 41.7
percent over 1992. Chief among these products were aircraft,
automobiles, textile machinery, machine tools, telephone
exchange machines, and construction and mining equipment.
Most of the increase in imports consisted of steel, refining oil,
steel billet and forging, and iron ore. Demand for these products
reflects China's rapid industrial growth.

China's top trading partner in 1993 was Japan, displacing
Hong Kong: Japan was followed by Hong Kong, the United
States, the EU, Taiwan, South Korea, Russia, Singapore, Austra-
lia, and Canada.

Foreign investment is rushing into China. By the end of 1993,
China approved a total of 173,975 foreign-invested projects with

$217.22 billion in contracted direct investment and $56.91 billion in utilized investment. In 1993 alone, China approved 83,265 foreign direct investment (FDI) projects with a total contracted value of $110.85 billion. Utilized direct investment reached $25.76 billion. The total amount of foreign investment in 1993 equaled total investment during the entire 14-year period since 1979.

Besides its unprecedented magnitude, foreign investment in China has other new characteristics:

- China has more capital sources than ever before. More than 100 countries and areas have invested in China.

- China's interior has attracted more foreign investment. Cities such as Wuhan, Chengdu, Chongqing, and Xian have attracted large amounts of foreign investment.

- Many projects now involve capital-intensive or technology-intensive industries such as electronics, machinery, telecommunications, and chemicals. Increasing investment has gone into energy and infrastructure projects.

- Average investment per project is larger. Many well-known multinational companies have come to China with numerous capital investment projects; average project size is now about $46 million.[4]

In summary, China's economic performance in recent years has improved markedly. Its development reflects the reconciliation between the openness of economic reform and the desire to maintain social stability. The development process has not been completely smooth; rapid economic growth has caused many problems, some of them quite serious. To achieve smooth and stable development and to avoid old evils such as economic overheating, China paradoxically must enhance its macroeconomic control while implementing reforms more quickly.

3

Problems of Economic Development

In the late 1970s, Deng Xiaoping stated that China's per capita income should reach $1,000 by the end of the century.[5] This greatly improved living standard would move China out from among the global poor to become a middle-income country. Accepted by the 12th Congress of the CCP in 1982, this goal was to be reached in three phases: During the 1980s, China should double its GNP; by the year 2000, China should double its GNP again to realize a fourfold increase; and, by the year 2050, China should approach the living standards of middle advanced countries. Since 1982, China's main domestic economic task has been to implement policies to attain these goals.

By 1990, China's GNP had exceeded its goal to double 1980 economic output. Because of economic difficulties such as China's irrational industrial structure, the low efficiency of state-owned enterprises, and the slow pace of economic reform, China's government decided that a growth rate of 6 percent would be adequate to increase China's GNP fourfold by the year 2000.

In spring 1992, however, Deng Xiaoping changed this projection. His speech given in southern China emphasized that China should further accelerate its development. In October 1992, the 14th Congress of the CCP announced that China would strive for an 8 percent to 9 percent annual increase in GNP.

Difficulty of Supporting High Growth Rates

Deng Xiaoping's speech stimulated overall economic development beginning in 1992. A high growth rate needs substantial supporting investment. In 1992, full social [total] investment in fixed assets increased by 42.6 percent; in the first half of 1993, this figure shot up by 61 percent. Even after cooling down in the second half of the year, total investment growth reached 50.6 percent.

China's financial problems limit its ability to sustain a long period of rapid growth. From 1990 to 1993, the annual rate of

Table 3.1
Revenue, Income, and Investment as a
Percentage of Gross Measures, 1985–1993

Year	Fiscal revenue / GNP	Fiscal revenue / National income	Revenue for investment / Total revenue	Full social investment / National income
1985	21.81	26.59	47.95	36.23
1986	23.31	28.76	54.63	–
1987	20.96	25.44	53.18	–
1988	18.68	22.39	53.16	38.31
1989	18.43	22.37	48.69	31.40
1990	18.72	23.03	46.68	30.93
1991	17.84	21.80	44.55	33.27
1992	17.28	21.80	39.64	38.84
1993	16.30	20.55	38.54	47.54

Source: Adapted from tables 2.1 and 2.2.

increase of full social investment in fixed assets reached 31.1 percent, outpacing the 9.6 percent average GNP growth rate.

In 1993, the ratio of full social investment in fixed assets to GDP was 37.7 percent, the ratio to national income 47.5 percent (see table 3.1); both figures were higher than during the 1980s.

Long-term, large-scale investment created severe problems for China for five related reasons. First, a high investment rate caused government revenue to decrease. In China, the ratio of fiscal revenue to GNP fell from 23.31 percent in 1986 to 16.30 percent in 1993, and the ratio to national income fell from 28.76 percent in 1986 to 20.55 percent in 1993; both are record lows. The ratio of capital investment from revenue to fiscal revenue also dropped from 54.63 percent in 1986 to only 38.54 percent in 1993 (table 3.1).

Second, many banks have had to borrow money illegally from each other; and many nonfinancial units, stimulated by high returns, have begun lending and borrowing money. These illegal businesses caused confusion in the financial sector, and the total amount of currency in circulation increased rapidly. In the first half of 1993, the overall capital investment of China increased by 61 percent, far exceeding GNP growth.

Third, investment was imbalanced as growth in the real estate sector reached as high as 144 percent. Nonproductive investment led to a capital shortage and, consequently, caused disarray in the financial sector. Despite low demand, office buildings, luxury houses, apartments, and other nonproductive projects absorbed over one-third of total capital investment. Some large projects eventually lay vacant.

Economic zones also absorbed large amounts of capital. Because little thought and planning had gone into the purpose of these zones and their sources of investment, technology, and supply, much land was wasted.

In contrast, investment in several basic sectors—energy, raw materials, and agriculture—lagged. Transportation is an important exception. In the first half of 1993, investment in energy, raw materials, and agriculture increased only 18.1 percent, 51.9 percent, and 28.6 percent respectively. This imbalance in investment exacerbated supply bottlenecks already affecting China's economy, fueling inflation as prices for uncontrolled commodities were bid up.

Fourth, long-term, large-scale investment caused shortages of production material and high inflation. In the first half of 1993, the average price for production materials increased by 44.7 percent over the previous year. Steel, cement, and timber prices doubled. Average inflation in urban areas was 13.5 percent in 1993. In 35 metropolitan areas, the inflation rate reached 17.4 percent.

Central government revenues are declining because

- tax reductions and exemptions were applied to many state-owned businesses;

- many local governments decided unilaterally to reduce or exempt local businesses from taxes;

- local governments provided many benefits to foreign investors at the expense of central government interests;

- the central government's contract system of taxation reduced almost all income tax due from state-owned enterprises because these firms were required to pay taxes only if they earned a profit; and

- tariffs were reduced to stimulate trade.

These developments led to disorder in the tax system as well as loss of revenue. Between 1991 and 1992, income tax revenues decreased 26 percent and, in the first half of 1993, decreased 26.4

percent again compared with the same period in 1992. From January to June 1993, tariff reductions increased by 21 percent over reductions in the same period of 1992. Tax evasion was widespread, in both private businesses and state-owned enterprises. An estimated 50 percent to 60 percent of China's state-owned enterprises and collectives and about 90 percent of its private businesses evade taxes. The central government's fiscal deficit became increasingly serious as government revenues decreased and expenditures increased.

From January to June 1993, government revenue increased by only 1.45 percent compared with 12.5 percent for the same period the year before. The balance on the government books was only about 2 billion yuan in the first half of 1993, about 17 billion yuan less than the same period in 1992. The central government's ability to adjust and control the economy had clearly decreased.

Implications for China's Economy

The foregoing problems also contributed to five economic challenges that face China:

The number of state-owned enterprises that are losing money is increasing. The low efficiency of state-owned enterprises has long been a major problem. Although China's rapid economic growth in the first half of 1993 stimulated growth in state-owned enterprises, it did not solve the enterprises' fundamental problems.

In 1993, about 60 percent of China's state-owned enterprises were operating at or near a deficit. By the end of that year, more than 50 percent of state-owned enterprises in many provinces were losing money. Since 1988, despite heavy government protection, more than 800 state-owned enterprises have gone bankrupt.

Of the enterprises losing money, the share of large and midsize state-owned enterprises increased to an unprecedented 28.5 percent in 1993 from 26.1 percent in 1990. In terms of value, 1993 was a record year: losses reached 37.69 billion yuan, four times higher than losses in 1988. The ratio of losses by large and midsize state-owned enterprises to total losses jumped in 1993 to 61.3 percent from 54.1 percent in 1990.

Most unprofitable enterprises were concentrated in the coal, petroleum and gas exploration, textiles, chemicals, machinery, and food processing sectors. They accounted for about 55.9 percent of the total losses of large and midsize enterprises. These losses affected not only government revenues but also worker incomes. For extended periods, many firms were unable to pay employees—with dangerous implications for stability.

Cost increases were the main reason for these losses. Rapid economic growth led to energy and raw material shortages, which in turn increased prices for these items. Price increases for inputs were on average much higher than price increases for outputs. For instance, in 1992, although output prices rose a record 24 percent, prices for energy and raw materials grew 35.1 percent, also a record high.

Another reason for losses by state-owned enterprises was inventory buildup. Inventories grew as sales fell, partly due to the government's tightening of loans and reduced growth rates and partly because many products were unsalable.

By the end of 1993, the value of inventories rose more than 30 percent over 1992 to 164.6 billion yuan. The large amount of inventory aggravated the shortage of capital and caused the so-called triangular debts. For example, by the end of 1993, the net amount of accounts receivable reached 256 billion yuan, 53 percent more than the previous year.

A third reason for losses by state-owned enterprises was the rapid increase in interest expenditures. Since 1983, China has sought to eliminate free capital distribution for state-owned enterprises. Enterprises must now obtain capital from banks rather than from government revenues. But in recent years, business expansion has made bank loans difficult to get, causing steep increases in interest burdens. By the end of 1993, the ratio of interest to total profit reached 59 percent, a figure three times higher than it was in 1988.

Finally, as discussed earlier, state-owned firms face problematic pricing constraints. If prices of inputs increase more rapidly than the prices their products command in the marketplace, the firms confront large losses. This has especially affected industries related to agriculture—agricultural machinery and chemical fertilizers. The profit rate of these two industries was only 3.3 percent, while their bank loan interest rates exceeded 10 percent. Many large firms have had to fill government orders at zero profit prices because capital shortages mean government departments do not have enough budgeted funds to pay full price to suppliers.

Table 3.2
Average Annual GNP Growth in China's Three Areas, 1979–1992
(in percentages)

Area	1979–1980	1981–1988	1989–1991	1992
East China	4.64	11.08	5.76	18.37
Central China	5.53	10.83	3.48	11.58
West China	5.00	10.77	6.11	9.23

Source: Adapted from *China Industrial Economics Research* (Beijing), no. 3 (1994), 28.

Economic disparities between the coast and the interior are widening.[6]   Since the 1980s, the economic disparities between China's interior and coastal areas have expanded gradually. In terms of GNP growth rate, the east grew more rapidly than the central region and the west. In 1992, the east's GNP grew by 18.37 percent over 1991, but the central region's increased by only 11.58 percent and the west's by only 9.23 percent. Growth rates for both the center and the west increased less than the national average of 13 percent (see table 3.2).

Differences among the three areas have increased; growth patterns have changed. From 1981 to 1988, growth was almost the same countrywide. In the late 1970s, growth was fastest in the central region, slowest on the coast.

Differences in regional shares of national GNP among eastern, central, and western China were clear. China's productivity has been shifting to the east from the interior, a shift that began with the country's economic reform and openness. The east increased its percentage of national GNP from 52.50 percent in 1978 to 56.55 percent in 1992. The share of GNP of the central provinces decreased from 31 percent to 27.95 percent between 1979 and 1992, and the western provinces' share decreased from 16.5 percent to 15.5 percent during the same period (see table 3.3).

China's interior, especially western China, is an area where minority nationalities live. Economic disparities could cause social instability and lead to separatist movements—a disaster that China wants to avoid.

In terms of per capita GNP, differences among the three areas are also evident. In 1978, per capita GNP was 457.4 yuan in the east, 310.3 yuan in the central region, and 254.0 yuan in the west,

Table 3.3
GNP Distribution by Area, Selected Years, 1978–1992
(in percentages)

Year	East China	Central China	West China
1978	52.50	31.00	16.50
1980	52.17	31.31	16.52
1986	53.10	30.90	16.00
1989	54.43	29.83	15.74
1991	54.90	28.79	16.31
1992	56.55	27.95	15.50

Source: Adapted from *China Industrial Economics Research* (Beijing), no. 3 (1994), 28.

Table 3.4
Per Capita GNP of China's Three Areas, Selected Years, 1978–1992
(in yuan)

Area	1978	1980	1986	1989	1991	1992
East China	457.4	488.3	860.7	1,098.7	1,192.6	1,398.9
Central China	310.3	336.0	579.6	696.9	721.6	796.3
West China	254.0	274.3	463.2	568.0	640.9	692.0

Source: Adapted from *China Industrial Economics Research* (Beijing), no. 3 (1994), 29.

yielding a ratio of 1:0.68:0.56. In 1992, the per capita GNP grew to 1,398.9 yuan in the east, 796.3 yuan in the central region, and 692.0 yuan in the west; this ratio was 1:0.57:0.49, which highlights growing regional disparities (see table 3.4).

One important reason for growing regional differences is that eastern China has attracted an overwhelming proportion of capital investment, including state capital, in recent years. For instance, in 1981, 45.9 percent of state capital was invested in the east, 18.0 percent in the central region, and 17.5 percent in the west; but, by 1992, the proportion became 54.6 percent in the east, 24.6 percent in the center, and 15.5 percent in the west (non-region specific state investment accounted for the balance).

Foreign investment was also largely centered in the east. From 1990 to 1992, China as a whole attracted $25.3 billion in real utilized capital. The east took about $22.8 billion, or 90.1 percent of total foreign investment. The central and western regions attracted only $1.74 billion and $0.76 billion, 6.9 percent and 3 percent respectively, of total foreign investment.[7]

One important way to maintain China's unity and prosperity is to provide enough economic aid to reduce differences in regional living standards. Weak central revenues, however, reduce the central government's ability to maintain economic equity among these areas. A government must be strong both politically and economically.

Frictions between the central government and local governments are increasing. Disorder in the areas of monetary policy and taxation caused sharp differences between China's central government and the local governments and undermined their relations because of differing interests and limited capital sources.

From late 1992 through spring 1993, both local and central governments demanded capital to fuel high investment growth. Large-scale interbank lending and borrowing appeared for the first time in China. Large amounts were lent for long-term investment without regard for borrower creditworthiness. Many local government leaders tried to borrow as much as they could to create new local business and to demonstrate their abilities and contributions to local development.

The ratio of central government revenue to GNP has continually decreased—from 26.7 percent in 1979, to 21.8 percent in 1985, to only 16.3 percent in 1993. As a result, the financial position of the central government has become relatively weaker, and relations between local governments and the central government have deteriorated.

Differences in personal income are widening. In recent years, unfair income allocation has become a serious issue in China. The gap between rich and poor has widened since the 1980s. Urban residents earned 70 percent more than rural residents in 1985 and over 120 percent more in 1991. The salary differential is apparent even in state-owned businesses; salaries in China's interior are only 75 percent as large as salaries on the coast.

Salaries also vary by ownership. In 1986, salaries in private businesses were 112 percent greater than salaries in state-owned businesses, and salaries in joint ventures were 15 percent greater than salaries in state-owned businesses. In 1991, these differences widened to 183 percent for private businesses compared with state-owned businesses and 40 percent for joint ventures compared with state enterprises.

The income gap between the top 10 percent and the bottom 10 percent of wage earners in China expanded from 4.6 times in

1991 to 4.8 times in 1992. Fifty million families in China, 2 percent of total families, have an income of more than 10,000 yuan per year. Among this group, about 5,000 families earn more than 1 million yuan and about 200 families earn more than 10 million yuan. In contrast, in 1991, per capita income in 9.4 percent of peasant families was less than 300 yuan. Per capita income of about 20 million rural people was only 150.80 yuan. Among 140 million urban residents, 7 million families had a monthly per capita income of only 62.19 yuan.[8]

In 1993, large-scale investment caused personal income to increase rapidly; 1993 was the best year for personal income growth in recent years. Average income nationwide reached 2,336.5 yuan, a real increase of 8.8 percent over 1992. Personal income in the east rose to 2,878.0 yuan; in the central region it reached 1,886.8 yuan; and in the west it was 2,045.1 yuan.

Absolute income in the central region and the west is below the national average. Highest and most rapidly growing incomes are in coastal areas. The five provinces and cities with the highest personal incomes are Guangdong at 4,227.2 yuan, Shanghai at 4,057.4 yuan, Zhejiang at 3,370.9 yuan, Beijing at 3,296.0 yuan, and Hainan at 2,774.4 yuan. The provinces and cities with the greatest growth of personal income over 1992 levels were Shanghai at 42.8 percent, Zhejiang at 39.6 percent, Beijing at 39.4 percent, Guangxi at 38.5 percent, and Guangdong at 34.3 percent.

Both regional differences and family differences in personal income are widening. According to a survey covering the year 1993, the average per capita income in the highest 10 percent of families was 4,502.0 yuan, an increase of 35.5 percent over 1992; the average per capita income in the lowest 10 percent of families was only 1,180.3 yuan, an increase of only 21 percent above 1992.

The number of families with a decreasing income has grown from 31 percent to 38 percent in 1993. Inflation directly affected 20.7 percent of these families, and 17.8 percent suffered for other reasons such as lost corporate profits.

High inflation is continuing.   Because of rampant investment and excessive growth in currency circulation in 1993, inflation has remained at a high level. According to estimates, 1993 average inflation was higher than it was the previous year—15 percent nationwide and 25 percent to 30 percent in 35 large cities. Retail price inflation in 1994 reached 24.2 percent; China's inflation target for 1995 is 15 percent.

In summary, capital shortages put China in a dilemma: should China slow inflation or increase the scale of investment to stimulate the vitality of state-owned enterprises? To control inflation, China must tighten loans and allow large numbers of state-owned enterprises to go bankrupt. But a large number of state-owned enterprises will suffer, endangering society. Workers who lose income would be a destabilizing factor, and the consequences could be dire.

On the other hand, if China tries to save state-owned enterprises, it will have to continue funneling funds to them. State-owned firms would receive loans and would operate their businesses, but China would face out-of-control inflation and the risk of social instability.

4

Effects of Economic Reform on State-Owned Enterprises

China has begun to reform its economic system and has made great progress since 1979 in developing its commercial market, or non-state sector, and increasing its openness. Fifteen years of reform and openness, however, have not completely changed China's old economic system. Its market system has not taken shape as quickly as some people expected; although compatible with the former planned economy, the areas that have not been reformed are unsuitable to a market system. The resulting problems have raised barriers to deepening the reform and completing the formation of China's market economy. Further reforms in taxation, monetary policy, foreign exchange, and investment have become an urgent task.

Problems of the Original Economic System

Fiscal Issues. Fiscal authority in the planned economy was based on the government's power to tightly control product prices and the monopoly position of state-owned enterprises. This strict control allowed the state to collect almost all profits from enterprises through taxation. This highly centralized tax system gave local governments and state-owned enterprises no incentive to improve productivity.

Serious reforms carried out since 1979 have given rights to both local governments and state-owned enterprises to create initiatives. The central government and local governments agreed to a compact that required the latter to remit a certain amount or percentage of profit they collected, leaving the remainder to be used at local governments' discretion. This "contract system on sharing revenue" or "tax farming system" was also applied to state-owned enterprises.

After 15 years of reform, however, China's fiscal situation still has severe problems. First, because the government's tax base depended almost totally on state-owned enterprises, the tax base was relatively narrow. With the proliferation of the non-state sector, taxes collected only from state-owned enterprises were insufficient. Because the central government collected taxes through local governments, there was no guarantee that the central government would receive enough revenue.

Second, taxing different regions, different industrial sectors, and different products at different rates was distortional and caused unfair tax burdens. It also undermined efforts to narrow income disparities among different regions and social groups. Economic disparities among different regions grew.

Finance.   In the planned economy, banks functioned not as real banks but as government cashiers. They provided capital to enterprises according to the central government's financial plan. Although the People's Bank of China (PBC), the central bank, and other banks were separated in 1984, their basic function was unchanged. Because these banks had no independent authority or responsibility, they made loans with little concern for commercial considerations.

In spite of the 1984 changes, the PBC still has insufficient independent decision-making authority. In addition to its basic function of stabilizing currency in circulation, its role is to support economic development and rescue unprofitable state-owned enterprises.

Another problem persists because of the PBC's unchanged administrative structure, which allows local governments to interfere with the bank at each administrative level. As local governments sought accelerated development, the bank was obligated to provide capital indiscriminately—a major cause of China's overheated economy.

In one county of Hunan Province, for example, the vice county magistrate ordered the president of the local bank branch to turn over the bank's seal so the magistrate could issue letters of credit at will. It was common for local officials to force bankers to provide loans to favored projects.

The PBC still depends on administrative means—quotas—to control or adjust currency in circulation rather than on interest rate adjustments. Because quotas are a soft restraint at each level of government and can break down, they are often meaningless.

The central bank has commercial interests in addition to its governmental functions; its discipline sometimes is compromised as it seeks profits rather than implementing governmental currency policies. These activities cause the central bank to favor easing rather than tightening currency controls.

Commercial banks have also experienced problems. They are not yet true commercial banks because they must undertake governmental policy tasks at the same time that they pursue their own self-interest.

Finally, the implementation of a dual interest rate system brought more trouble. Interest rates on loans and deposits were below market rates, stimulated borrowing, and caused overinvestment. Dual interest rates were a major reason for corruption as those with access to cheaper capital exploited the interest rate differential.

Foreign Exchange. Under the planned economic system, the central government tightly controlled foreign exchange. All hard currency earned by enterprises had to be remitted to the central bank, and the government had to approve all hard currency expenditures. The government set the exchange rate, not according to the market but according to the rate the government needed to facilitate imports. The official exchange rate, therefore, was much lower than the market rate.

The low exchange rate benefited enterprises that had access to hard currency because it made imports inexpensive. This highly centralized system also benefited government because it enabled it to allocate the limited hard currency. The system, however, did not encourage enterprises to earn hard currency.

Beginning in 1979, reforms in foreign exchange involved creating a dual exchange rate system. The official rate was much lower than the market rate. The second rate was close to the market rate and was used at foreign exchange swap centers. Enterprises had to bear the higher yuan cost of imported products. In an effort to mitigate this situation, a "contract system on sharing hard currency" was implemented between the central government and local governments and between the government and enterprises: after local governments or enterprises remitted certain amounts or percentages of hard currency earned, they could keep the rest for their own use.

Some new problems appeared after the dual exchange rate reform was undertaken. First, the foreign exchange market was not connected nationwide and was blocked by each local government. Local governments also retained hard currency and tried to use it in their own jurisdictions. Because the demand for capital and the rate of return have differed from region to region, limited hard currency is attracted to the coastal areas. For example, in Shenzhen, a Special Economic Zone on the coast, the demand for foreign exchange and the rate of return are higher than in China's interior. To prevent the outflow of hard currency to other areas, local governments in the interior have blocked the development of foreign exchange markets.

Implementation of the dual rate structure actually created three exchange rates in China. One was the official rate, the lowest rate of exchange. The middle rate was the rate for the foreign exchange swap centers. The third was the market rate, which made hard currency expensive but which is also illegal. The three-tier system contributed to many problems such as corruption, unfair competition between state-owned and non-state-owned firms, especially foreign invested firms, and inefficiency in state-owned enterprises.

The contract system on sharing hard currency decreased the central government's macroeconomic control. Because China's foreign exchange reserves include the bank's working capital, residential deposits, and local government and enterprise deposits, the real amount of foreign exchange at the disposal of the central government is limited. The central government's ability to adjust foreign exchange reserves is also limited to administrative means, which are often inefficient.

Investment. China's investment system is tightly linked to enterprise management, finance, monetary policy, pricing, and material management. Reforms in these related areas must be promoted if the investment system is to be changed. As a developing country, China plans large-scale construction and technology transformation for existing enterprises, but these plans require efficient investment and an effective management structure. Problems hindering the growth of investment and the readjustment of investment structures and contributing to irresponsibility and corruption include

- the lack of restraints on investment risk. Investments undertaken without serious planning are common and severely obstruct economic development;

- the lack of effective management of mass investment and the inability to change the mass investment situation;

- pricing and monetary policies that discourage banks from financing investment in basic industries and infrastructure; and,

- the legal system.

The Economic Reform Program

Deng Xiaoping's comments in the South of China in spring 1992 created another push for economic development. However, because existing economic systems could not meet the needs of economic development and openness, China's economy overheated.

Economic reform once again became an urgent issue. To cool the economy and adjust the disorder, the central government adopted "sixteen countermeasures" to enhance macroeconomic control. The CCP mandated that the central government draw up a plan to establish a market system by the end of the century. On January 1, 1994, China implemented important reforms in taxation, finance, monetary policy, foreign exchange, and investment in fixed assets.

Tax Reform.   Tax reform attempted to restructure the tax system, simplify and consolidate the taxation system, allocate tax collection and distribution rights between the central government and local governments, establish a suitable tax system for a market economy, and promote fair competition among the enterprises.

First, the government implemented a new tax system, based on a value-added tax (VAT), a consumption tax, and a sales tax. This new system applies to all Chinese and foreign-invested businesses. The VAT will cover all types of commodity transactions, including production, wholesale, retail, and import. Sixteen tax categories were reduced to two: one is the basic tax rate (17 percent of total added value), and the other is the reduced rate (13 percent of total added value). Taxes were levied according to receipts. For some special goods such as cigarettes, alcohol, cosmetics, and gasoline, the new system includes a consumption tax on top of the VAT.

Second, the government unified the income tax for Chinese firms and simplified the income tax for different types of firms. It abolished the fund for energy and transportation and the fund for budget adjustment that applied a special tax to Chinese firms. In the future, different tax rates levied on Chinese firms and foreign firms will be unified into one rate.

Third, the reforms are expected to unify the personal income tax, the personal income adjusting tax, and the single property business income tax. Taxation begins at 800 yuan on a progressive schedule.

Finally, reforms were expected to ensure completion of the taxation process, creation of a national tax-collecting agency, and creation of a local government tax-collecting agency. Central government taxes and taxes shared by the central government and local governments will be collected by the national tax-collecting agency; the local use taxes will be collected by the local tax-collecting agency.

Center-Province Fiscal Reform.   The goal of fiscal reform is to implement a "tax division system" to replace the "contract system on sharing revenue" between the central and provincial governments. The "tax division system" would

- identify the responsibilities of each level of government, including province, county, city, and town, and divide the functions among different levels of government;

- identify the scale of fiscal expenditures based on these different functions;

- divide taxes in two parts—central government revenue and local government revenue—and ensure that the central government receives 60 percent of total tax revenue; and

- create a tax transfer system to allocate central government revenue to local governments and to adjust regional economic differences.

These goals will be reached in two steps. The first involves changing the expenditures of each level of government and delineating the sources of revenue. Beginning in 1994, receipts from the customs tax and the consumption tax go to the central government; receipts from the sales tax, real estate tax, and personal income tax go to local governments; receipts from the business income tax, resources tax, and VAT are shared by the central government and local governments. A reimbursement system will be created by which the central government will shift revenues based on 1993 benchmark figures to designated local governments.

The second step includes reassessing the functions of each level of government and establishing standards for government expenditures. In addition, the central government will transfer certain monies to each local government according to its basic responsibilities.

Banking Reform.   Monetary reform should separate the functions of commercial banks from the functions of the central bank; establish a financial system formed mainly by state-owned commercial banks and by various monetary institutions; produce an open, competitive banking system; and create an orderly, well-managed currency market.

If a strong central banking system is to be created, the PBC must become a real central bank. The Third Plenum of the 14th National Congress of the CCP issued "Decisions on Some Problems of Establishing a Socialist Market Economic System" in which it stated that the main task of the central bank is to maintain macroeconomic stability.

Secondary responsibilities of the central bank are regulating and managing various monetary institutions, maintaining monetary order, and implementing monetary policies independently under the leadership of the State Council. Monetary management should consist of setting the reserve requirements and the rediscount rate, opening business to the public rather than simply controlling loans, controlling the total amount of currency in circulation, and ensuring the stability of the currency.

To accomplish these objectives, the government should restructure the central bank. It must change the PBC's functions by centralizing the right to issue and recall basic currency and adjust the scale of loans. The government should also abolish the contract system of sharing profits between local banks and the central bank; the central bank system should adhere to worldwide banking practices and customs. Branch offices should be restructured and set up throughout China; subsidiary offices at the city and regional levels should function as inspection agencies that inspect and manage monetary institutions and the monetary market.

To establish a viable monetary system would require transforming existing banks into real commercial banks that can separate commercial functions from policy functions. Ties must be cut between policy loan functions and basic credit functions. Only the central bank should control adjustments in the money supply.

Policy banks, under government guidance, currently issue loans for long-term construction projects with low profit potential that benefit the entire society; loans are provided for countrywide infrastructure projects, basic industries, development of high technologies, import and export credits for designated capital goods, and agriculture development. Policy banks are composed of development banks such as the Import and Export Credit Bank and the Agriculture Development Bank, whose capital resources come from economic construction capital in the form of revenue, financially secured bonds, and financial bonds issued for banking institutions.

In an open, competitive commercial bank system, policy banks must be separated from other banks, and the remaining three major state banks—the Business Bank, the Bank of China, and the Agriculture Bank—should become commercial banks immediately. These banks must follow modern banking rules: They should operate independently, assume responsibility for their own profits or losses as well as their own business development, and assess and deal with risk. Banks must be free to deal with any number of business sectors rather than be limited to only certain sectors.

The internal structure of each bank should be set up according to its own commercial needs, with each bank responsible for its own management and operating capital. The central bank would lend only to the headquarters of each commercial bank. The main offices of each commercial bank would be responsible for the bank's capital flow and liabilities. A board of supervisors accountable to the State Council would be set up in each bank to inspect bank operations, keep records, assess the achievements of bank officers, and suggest personnel changes, rewards, or punishments.

In addition to major state-owned banks, other commercial banks such as the Agriculture Cooperation Bank of China, the Communication Bank, the Zhongxin Industrial Bank, the Guangda Bank, and some regional commercial banks such as the Guangdong Province Bank would operate independently and compete with one another under the inspection of the central bank. Such banks, especially cooperation banks in both rural and urban areas, should be developed because China's market is so large.

Two other major state-owned banks—the People's Construction Bank and the Investment Bank of China—would also become long-term credit commercial banks after their policy functions are transferred to other policy banks.

China will promote the formation of capital markets with market interest rates by establishing a nationwide market linked through electronic networks. All financial institutions must be approved to enter this market and to participate in some central bank functions such as rediscounting, issuing bonds, and accommodation.

Restrictions on yields on bonds issued by banks and enterprises would be abolished gradually to settle at market-determined rates. For the time being, the PBC will adjust interest rates in response to market signals and allow banks to float interest rates on deposits and loans. Once capital markets stabilize, controls on interest rates will be lifted.

Foreign Exchange Reform. The ultimate goal of foreign exchange reform is to make the Chinese yuan completely convertible. China must take two steps to reach this goal: abolish the dual foreign exchange rate system to make the yuan convertible under certain conditions, and abolish government control of capital flows to make the yuan completely convertible.

On January 1, 1994, the Chinese government combined the dual foreign exchange rates and allowed a floating rate based on market supply and demand. Each day, the PBC publishes floating exchange rates for major foreign currencies citing the previous day's rates. Each bank deals in foreign currency within a range regulated by the central bank.

China has also abolished both the approval system for hard currency to import goods and the mandatory hard currency deposit system for export earnings. Anyone who needs to import can now change hard currency with a certificate.

Investment System Reform. After 15 years of study, China will implement the following changes:

- Change the investment allocation from the government plan to the open market. Most competitive investment projects—namely, projects promising high returns—will be financed by enterprises and private firms that will make their own investment decisions according to market demand. The government will withdraw from these types of projects but will ensure the continuation of large infrastructure construction projects of national importance through the National Development Bank, government revenues and bonds, foreign borrowing, and bank deposits. Some projects started by the central government or local governments should be sold to enterprises gradually.

The main task for government in these types of projects is to enhance the flow of information and policy guidance.

- Regulate government investment and concentrate capital to build national projects. The task of government is to sponsor basic projects such as infrastructure, basic industries, and high technology industries.

- Divide responsibilities among the central government and local governments according to the beneficiary of investment. Local infrastructure and basic construction, including transportation, mail and telecommunications, energy, agriculture, and city infrastructure, will be the responsibility of the local government, but local governments will be permitted to attract private capital. The central government will provide some subsidiary investment to the less developed regions.

- Fund social benefit projects such as higher education, culture, health care, environmental protection, and sports from local government revenues. Defense projects will be borne by the central government. Funding of projects enhancing private consumption will be by individuals.

- Open certain industries, especially energy, transportation, and services, to foreign investment and participation.

The Positive Effects of China's Economic Reforms

How have the new reforms that were implemented in the early part of 1994 affected the Chinese economy, especially state-owned businesses? Of the five reforms discussed above, only investment reform is not considered because it has yet to be implemented.

Theoretically, the reforms have had a positive impact. Since China decided to become a socialist market economy, it has needed to create a complete market climate for all types of business enterprises—state-owned, collective, private, foreign, and joint ventures—so that all can compete equally and fairly. Government should separate its public administrative functions from its commercial functions, but it also needs to create new indirect controls and methods to regulate business activities.

Without such reforms, a modern market system in China will be impossible.

Tax Reform.

- China has created a financial system and a tax system promoting a unified market and financial stability. To accomplish this, China has pursued reasonable income distribution and has regulated relations between the government and enterprises, between the government and individuals, and between the central government and local governments.

- Government revenue is central to the process of national income distribution.

- The new tax division system has overcome China's traditional linkage between local government and all tax revenues collected in the locality. Local government has always tried to protect its interest without concern for the central government's interest. Now, however, the interests of both the central government and local governments are protected through mutual identification and sharing of revenues.

- The new unified tax rate has reduced the burden on state-owned enterprises. Before tax reform, different corporate structures had different tax rates. The corporate income tax rate for a state-owned firm was fixed at 55 percent of its total income; the highest category designated in a progressive tax on income of collectives and private firms was fixed at 55 percent; joint ventures were tax free during the first three years and then paid a reduced tax rate for another two years before eventually paying regular progressive rates. Now there is one income tax rate: all firms, regardless of legal type, will pay 33 percent, although joint ventures continue to receive preferential treatment. In addition, the number of tax categories has been reduced from 32 to 18, resulting in a simplified tax system that makes it easy to determine obligations and to collect the taxes owed.

- Government revenue has increased since the new tax system was implemented. In the first six months of 1994, government revenue nationwide reached 197.94 billion yuan, an increase of 22.6 percent over the same period in 1993. Expenditures during the first six months of 1994 amounted to 197.33 billion yuan, an increase of 27 percent over the same period in 1993. China achieved a 610-million-yuan surplus.

Monetary Reform.

- Overissuance of currency ended in mid-1993. In the first half of 1994, a total of 8.3 billion yuan was reabsorbed; the total net reabsorbed currency was 661.1 billion yuan more than during the same period of 1993.

- Although resident deposits decreased in the first quarter of 1993, they have been increasing since July 1993. In 1993, there was a 321.8-billion-yuan deposit increase.

- The government cannot borrow money directly from banks to clear deficits, but it can issue bonds to raise cash. Although many people worried that government bonds would not sell, more than 100 billion yuan worth of government bonds were issued in 1994. By the end of July 1994, bonds worth 102.9 billion yuan had been sold to the public. Savings deposits did not decrease because almost all the bonds were purchased in cash.

Foreign Exchange Reform.

- The unified, market-based exchange rate creates a normal and transparent environment for all types of transactions.

- Corruption based on the dual exchange rates has ended.

- A normal and stable exchange rate has stimulated foreign trade and made China more attractive to foreign investors. In 1994, China's total exports reached $121 billion, an increase of 31.9 percent over 1993; imports reached $115.7 billion, an increase of 11.2 percent over 1993. Total trade was $236.7 billion.

- The unified exchange rate has created a barrier to imports because market-based exchange rates have raised the yuan price of imports.

- The foreign exchange rate has stabilized since the dual rate system was abolished. In June 1993 the swap rate dropped to $1.00 = 11 yuan, but since August 1993 it has increased to $1.00 = 8.70 yuan and stabilized at this level. During the first six months of 1994, the Chinese yuan even appreciated slightly to $1.00 = 8.50 yuan.

- The unified foreign currency market has actually contributed to China's foreign reserves. From January 1994 to April 1994, settlement of exchange was $7.3 billion, while sales of foreign exchange totaled $4.2 billion. During this time, foreign reserves increased $8 billion more than they had in early 1993.

- The quantity of foreign exchange has satisfied the needs of foreign-invested firms. For example, in April 1994 foreign-invested businesses purchased $135 million and HK$64 million in 19 foreign exchange transactions centers.

The Negative Effects of China's Economic Reforms

A regulated and relatively fair economic climate is always good for private business. Joint ventures have benefited the most from China's economic reforms because their priorities have not been changed. State-owned enterprises have experienced the greatest number of changes. The most severe negative impacts are from tax reform, foreign exchange reform, and foreign trade reform.

Tax Reform.   The 1994 tax reform created a rigid system under which enterprises cannot avoid taxes, creating a burden for many enterprises. Before reform, firms could pay less tax or avoid tax payments altogether because local governments could decide whether to reduce or remit their burden. Thus firms rarely paid as much as the central government required even though rates were set at 55 percent of income. The new taxation and new collection systems make it impossible, however, for local governments to continue to play favorites. Some enterprises in the chemical fertilizer, drug manufacture, and food processing industries believe their tax burden is unfair: although the prices of their products had not been freed and allowed to rise to market levels, they had to pay taxes on the same basis as other firms.

The potential losses facing many firms were realized once their taxes were paid; taxes even drove some firms toward bankruptcy. In the first two months of 1994, for example, state-owned firms in Nanjing had to pay a VAT of 126.7 million yuan, 36.88 million yuan more than during the same period in 1993, an increase of 41 percent. The number of money-losing firms is also increasing. In 1993, 82 out of a total of 196 firms lost money; by early 1994, the number had climbed to 109, 55.6 percent of the total firms. Collectives also suffered under the new tax system. In Nanjing in 1994, of 127 firms owned by 207 collectives, 61 percent lost money, an increase of 24.7 percent over 1993.

Although the income tax rate for private businesses has been reduced from 55 percent to 33 percent since 1994, in the past these firms actually paid a de facto rate of less than 17 percent. Thus the enterprise income tax in 1994 represented an increase of 214 percent. Businesses, especially the state firms, bear higher taxes than in the past.

Foreign Exchange Reform. Since the abolition of the official exchange rates, state firms have had to buy U.S. dollars at a higher rate. The cost of U.S. dollars has increased by approximately 50 percent. In general, because foreign currency is tightly controlled by the government, Chinese firms have to borrow foreign currency to import equipment or material. With the yuan's steep and rapid depreciation, firms must spend more local currency to buy hard currency to repay loans, a heavy burden. Many firms have "bottomless debt" status.

For example, the Jing-Jin Glass Shell Factory manufactures glass shells for tubes used in producing television sets. In 1984, the factory borrowed 150 million yuan (including U.S. dollars), imported a production line from Japan, and started production in 1986. The factory was a success: its products were of high quality, it earned high profits, and it possessed a high market share. But although the factory had repaid its lender 163 million yuan by the end of 1993, it still owed another 210 million yuan, more than it has had in returns, because of the rapid depreciation of the Chinese yuan. The factory had borrowed hard currency at $1.00 = 1.90 yuan and $1.00 = 2.80 yuan, and the cost to repay the loan has more than tripled. Consequently, the factory is carrying all the debts and falling into a "bottomless debt" position. This situation is not unique. Many firms that imported foreign equipment using hard currency at the former official rate now have to repay more in yuan terms than anticipated and have suffered as a result.

Foreign Trade Reform. Import barriers in China are higher than at any time in the past. Foreign exchange at market prices has in effect been a barrier to imports; and for Chinese enterprises, advantages in taxes and tariffs gained by importing foreign equipment have disappeared. For instance, state-owned firms in 14 open cities in the coastal areas at one time faced no tariffs on equipment imported for technological transformation. In 1994, the tariff on such goods was 7.5 percent to 10 percent of total value and was scheduled to rise to the full tariff of between 15 percent and 20 percent in 1995. In addition, the VAT rate for imported material, originally only 14 percent, has increased to 17 percent. Because of the higher exchange rate and the increase in tariffs, most Chinese firms cannot bear the cost of imports, and the total value of imports has decreased.

The current high cost of imports is one important reason why China had a trade surplus in 1994. In some places, such as Tianjin, there were no imports of equipment in the first half of 1994. In Shanghai, China's largest customs area, the value of imported equipment decreased by 51 percent between 1993 and 1994. Yet despite the serious negative impact of these charges on Chinese firms, foreign-invested businesses still have access to many tariff advantages; equipment imported by foreign-invested firms for their own use is tariff free, for example.

The economic reforms in China will create a fair climate for all enterprises and promote linkage to the world market, but state-owned enterprises will suffer because many of them cannot bear the attendant burdens. Because business profits have decreased, state revenue has declined, severely affecting the strength of the government's macroeconomic control. Inflation has also negatively affected the vitality of state-owned enterprises.

The most serious problem, however, is the appearance of a new imbalance in policy priorities: Because there has been no change in policies affecting the foreign investment sector, great contrasts are appearing between foreign-invested businesses and domestic businesses. The new taxation and tariff policies have forced domestic businesses to form joint ventures with foreign businesses to gain a share of the advantages.

Foreign businesses have rushed into China in the last two years, providing opportunities for Chinese firms, especially in coastal areas, to join with them. For example, in the chemical industry in Tianjin, about two-thirds of the state-owned firms have joined with foreign businesses. Other firms are continuing to seek foreign partners.

Because many well-managed state-owned businesses have joined with foreign businesses, the number of purely state-owned businesses is decreasing. Most of them are not turning a profit—an important reason why the proportion of money-losing state-owned businesses is increasing. Those that are commercially stronger have found foreign partners and are classified as joint ventures. If this trend continues, the remaining state-owned businesses will soon be in danger.

5

Openness and Utilizing Foreign Capital

It is no secret that China has attracted a large amount of foreign capital. The World Bank announced that China was the largest recipient of foreign capital in 1993, signing 83,423 foreign investment projects worth $122.68 billion with actual utilized investment of $36.77 billion—increases, respectively, of 70.7 percent, 76.7 percent, and 91.5 percent above 1992. For foreign investment projects, FDI amounted to $110.85 billion, 90.4 percent of total contracted investment. Actual utilized investment totaled $25.76 billion, 1.3 times more than the previous year.[9] Both the scale of utilized foreign investment and the rapid acceleration of foreign investment reached record highs.

By the end of 1993, cumulative foreign investment in China totaled $313.8 billion in contract terms and $135.6 billion in actual utilized terms. Out of these figures, contracted FDI equaled $221.3 billion and actual FDI reached $60.1 billion. This disbursed investment was 12.5 percent of full social capital investment in China. Foreign investment therefore has become an important source of capital for China.

In 1993, contracted foreign investment in coastal areas reached $94.4 billion, an increase of 78.6 percent above 1992, which amounted to 86.7 percent of the total contracted investment in China. Signatories in China's interior approved contracts worth $14.5 billion, an increase over 1992 of more than 110 percent; this amount was 13.1 percent of total investment in the PRC. The top 10 recipients of foreign investment were Guangdong, Jiangsu, Fujian, Shanghai, Shandong, Liaoning, Zhejiang, Guangxi, Hainan, and Beijing.

The size of foreign investment projects has grown. In 1993, for example, Guangdong Province had 700 projects and Fujian Province 280, each worth more than $100,000. The largest single project, a Hong Kong investment, was worth more than $600 million.

Hong Kong, Macao, and Taiwan were still the main sources of capital for mainland China. In 1993, Hong Kong and Macao invested in 50,608 projects worth a contracted $73.1 billion, up 71.8 percent from 1992. There were more than 10,000 projects from Taiwan worth $9.5 billion in contracted investment in 1993, registering respective one-year increases of 57.1 percent and 66.5 percent. In 1993, other countries that were large capital sources for China were the United States with $6.1 billion, an increase of 84 percent; Japan at $2.8 billion, an increase of 23.7 percent; Singapore at $2.79 billion, an increase of 160 percent; the United Kingdom (UK) at $1.9 billion, an increase of 520 percent; South Korea at $1.6 billion, an increase of 240 percent; Canada at $1.16 billion, an increase of 270 percent; Thailand at $1.06 billion, an increase of 45.6 percent; and Malaysia at $0.66 billion, an increase of 210 percent. Together, they accounted for 90.1 percent of contracted FDI in China in 1993.

By the end of 1993, the number of foreign-invested enterprises in China had reached 168,000, double that of 1992. These firms consisted of 108,000 joint ventures, 26,000 corporations, and 34,000 completely foreign-owned firms.

Benefits of Foreign Investment to China

Attracting foreign investment to China and promoting foreign-invested business in China are important to China's openness policy. Since 1979, when China improved its investment climate, foreign investment has continued to increase and to play an ever greater role. Now an inseparable part of the Chinese economy, foreign investment has

- *restructured ownership and China's new vitality.*   China's 150,000 foreign-invested firms actually shaped a new competitive strength in China and broke up state ownership. China is now an economy with state-owned, collective, private, foreign-invested, and joint venture enterprises. Having a competitive economy with different types of business ownership is an important factor in stimulating China's rapid development.

- *met China's capital needs.*   The ratio of foreign investment to China's social investment in fixed assets was an average of 2.5 percent in the 1980s, which grew to an average of about 6 percent during the first four years of the 1990s.

In 1992, foreign-invested businesses contributed 8 percent of China's GDP and 6 percent of the gross value of its industrial output.

- *introduced and promoted advanced technologies in China.* Because foreign-invested projects in China use advanced equipment and technologies, the gap between China and advanced countries in high technology has been reduced. Many products that could not be made in China in the past can now be produced and exported—for example, large telephone switch machines for commercial use made by joint ventures in China. Production of such goods as automobiles, color televisions, and aircraft has been improving rapidly in China because of foreign technology.

- *created job opportunities in China.* Foreign-invested businesses have absorbed 6 million laborers, reducing social pressures in China.

- *provided increased revenue for the Chinese government.* Foreign investment has become an important source of China's tax revenue. In 1992, foreign businesses paid taxes totaling 10.7 billion yuan, excluding customs tariffs, contributing 4 percent of government revenue. In the first half of 1993, these revenues reached 8.08 billion yuan, an increase of 65.9 percent above the same period in 1992.

- *increased China's exports.* Foreign firms have been important in developing China's export sector. The total value of external trade of China's foreign-invested enterprises reached $67.07 billion in 1993, according to statistics provided by the China Custom House, representing 34.3 percent of China's total imports and exports. Exports reached $25.24 billion, an increase of 45.4 percent above 1992. Exports of foreign-invested firms accounted for 27.5 percent of China's total exports in 1993, up from 20.4 percent in 1992.[10] Ninety-four percent of exports created by foreign businesses consisted of manufactured products.

- *brought appreciation of the market economy and managerial experience to China.* Foreign investment opened the minds of Chinese people and improved their appreciation of the market economy and the world market. Foreign firms trained many professionals in China who are now skilled at international business—a key factor although not quantifiable.

The challenge for China now is attracting additional foreign investment in the strongly competitive environment of East Asia and to make foreign investment more responsive to China's needs. The benefits to China of hosting foreign-invested businesses are evident. Openness is, and will remain, the correct policy for China and will continue to be promoted.

Regulating Foreign Investment: Resolving the Problems

Foreign capital is not a perfect source of capital for China. Some disadvantages and contradictions are appearing as the scale of investment expands.

One problem is that many foreign-invested firms are shams, existing only as signed contracts and introducing no new capital into China. Many Chinese firms, to take advantage of the tax and tariff policy benefits provided only to foreign-invested businesses, have made agreements with foreign companies for the use of their foreign names. But the foreign firms do not expend actual capital or make other investments. From 1979 to 1993, contracted foreign investment reached $221.3 billion in China, but actual utilized investment was only $60.1 billion, a mere 27 percent of total contracted investment. The ratio of actual utilized investment to contracted investment was 23 percent in 1993, down from 66 percent in 1986.

The fraudulent joint venture created by the textile department in one province is a typical example. To enjoy tax exemptions, the department contracted with and sent $100,000 to a British company, which turned around and invested the $100,000 in China as foreign investment. The Chinese company then enjoyed the tax benefits of a joint venture. For its participation, the British company received a $20,000 commission.

Attracting foreign investment has become an important measure of local leaders. A local leader who creates a joint venture can be promoted and receive a big bonus. This is another incentive for creating false joint ventures.

Another problem is tax evasion. To evade taxes, many foreign-invested firms falsify their accounts and do not report their real income. Although they appear to be losing money, they are increasing investment and expanding their business in China. In 1990, for example, Guangdong Province officials inspected 1,090 foreign-invested firms, 544 of which were apparently losing money, with losses totaling 3.33 billion yuan. One very successful joint venture in Shenzhen claimed a deficit that surpassed its registered capital; the department of taxation found the firm had made a false declaration to evade taxes. This phenomenon has spread throughout China.

Many foreign investors overcharge for the equipment they import. In one case, the reported cost of imported equipment was $68.86 million when the actual cost was $52.34 million. In general, the reported cost of equipment imported as foreign investment is 20 percent to 50 percent higher than the actual cost.

Some foreign investors even import obsolete machinery—junk—into China under the guise of investment. For example, a firm created a joint venture to develop garment accessories. Foreign investment, 43 percent of total investment, took the form of equipment—all of which was obsolete.

Infringement on the rights of workers in foreign-invested firms is becoming increasingly serious. Disputes between laborers and managers are occurring more frequently. According to a General Labor Union survey of 20 foreign-invested firms in 10 different cities of Guangdong Province, overtime work has become very prevalent: more than 60 percent of the employees received no vacation time, 34.7 percent were forced to work overtime, and 20.1 percent received no compensation for their extra work. Another example of infringement of workers' rights occurred in a Japanese joint venture luxury hotel in Shanghai when a guest reported that 1,000 yuan had been stolen; the foreign manager forced two Chinese waitresses to remove their clothes and inspected them illegally.

Many foreign firms also ignore labor safety standards. In 1993, the Health Department of Zhuhai city checked seven joint ventures and found levels of poisonous gas in the workshops eight to nine times higher than the world standard; in three toy-manufacturing firms, 81 people were poisoned, 4 of whom died and 8 of whom became crippled as a result of the poisoning.

On November 19, 1993, 84 girls received fatal burns in a workshop in Shenzhen; the supervisor, a Hong Kong national, had closed the windows and locked the doors. It was later determined that the accident had occurred solely because the firm ignored national safety and fire regulations. One month later, 63 workers died in a fire in Fuzhou; these workers lived one floor above the workshop, which had a manager from Taiwan.[11]

These tragic accidents shocked Chinese citizens, who began to wonder why China needs foreign investors. By conjuring comparisons to colonialists and arousing questions of morality, these accidents may be causing an aversion to foreign investors.

China's domestic market has absorbed much foreign capital. The cost of labor is low, and infrastructure development and the legal system are almost complete. Although foreign investment has played an increasingly important role in China's economic development, it has also introduced some critical problems that challenge not only China's economy but also the society's very foundation—its concepts of social value, morals, and democracy. China must balance the benefits and costs of foreign investment to determine a long-term strategic direction that will not be distorted by short-term benefits.

6

China's Economic and Foreign Relations

Linking China's Economy to East Asia

Since 1979, China's economy has depended on foreign suppliers for natural resources, advanced technology, and capital and on foreign markets for its exports. Total trade as a share of GNP has grown steadily from 12.8 percent in 1980 to 37.96 percent in 1992,[12] confirming China's increasing dependence on the global economy. But what is the economic relationship between China and East Asia? Specifically, what is the relationship between China and economic leaders in the Pacific region? Because the United States is very influential in East Asia, it will be included in this discussion.

The Asia-Pacific region has been the most important area for China's trade. The total value of China's imports and exports reached $165.61 billion in 1992, an increase of 22.1 percent over 1991. Of that trade, the Asia-Pacific region accounted for 80.4 percent. Trade with East Asia rose 21.7 percent, to $110.2 billion, representing 66.52 percent of total Chinese trade.

China's top four trading partners in 1992 were Hong Kong, Japan, the United States, and Taiwan. Taken together, they accounted for 64.9 percent of total Chinese foreign trade in 1992 (see table 6.1).

As trade relations developed, foreign investment flowed into China, mainly from the Pacific region. In 1992, foreign investors from the Asia-Pacific greatly increased the amount of capital they invested in China: investment from the Pacific region increased 126.1 percent to $14.24 billion and comprised 74.2 percent of foreign investment in China, up from 54.5 percent in 1991.

The bulk of investment came from Hong Kong and Macao, which increased their investments in China by 197.1 percent over 1991. Hong Kong and Macao supplied 45.3 percent of total foreign investment in China in 1992, up from 25.3 percent in 1991.

Table 6.1
China's Regional Trade, 1992
(in millions of U.S. dollars)

Geographic Areas	Total Value of Trade	% of Total	Total Export	Total Import	Partner Ranking
Total world	165,608.38	100.00	84,998.21	80,610.13	-
Total region	133,089.90	80.36	71,167.25	61,922.65	-
Asia	110,161.93	66.52	61,124.59	49,037.34	-
Hong Kong	58,050.30	35.05	37,512.22	20,538.08	1
Japan	25,380.09	15.33	11,699.37	13,680.72	2
Taiwan	6,579.02	3.97	698.04	5,880.98	4
South Korea	5,060.61	3.06	2,437.45	2,623.16	5
Singapore	3,267.05	1.97	2,030.84	1,236.21	6
Indonesia	2,025.58	1.22	471.43	1,554.15	9
Malaysia	1,475.11	0.89	645.44	829.67	10
Thailand	1,269.47	0.77	894.81	423.99	11
North Korea	696.57	0.42	541.11	155.46	12
Macao	694.10	0.42	528.68	165.42	13
Philippines	643.00	0.39	551.43	91.57	14
Vietnam	179.07	0.11	106.36	72.71	16
North America	20,073.99	12.12	9,247.23	10,826.76	-
United States	17,493.58	10.56	8,593.73	8,899.85	3
Canada	2,579.75	1.56	653.20	1,926.55	7
South Pacific	2,853.98	1.72	795.43	2,058.55	-
Australia	2,332.07	1.41	600.8	1,671.26	8
New Zealand	366.30	0.22	87.43	278.87	15
Other	155.61	0.09	47.19	108.42	16

Source: Adapted from *Statistical Yearbook of China, 1993*, pp. 638–640.

Investment from Taiwan also grew steadily, increasing 123.2 percent above that of the previous year; its portion of the total mainland foreign investment reached 5.5 percent in 1992, up from 4.1 percent in 1991. Japanese investment in China also grew rapidly, increasing 67.9 percent between 1991 and 1992. The United States maintained its relatively lower foreign investment profile in China, increasing its investment in 1992 by only 30.9 percent above 1991 (see table 6.2).

Multilateral lending organizations also channeled funds into China. The World Bank provided $1.097 billion in loans to China in 1992, representing 5.7 percent of total foreign capital inflows;

Table 6.2
China's Foreign Capital Inflows from the Asia-Pacific Region, 1992
(in millions of U.S. dollars)

Geographic Areas	Total	Foreign Loans	Direct Investment	% of Total	Partner Ranking
Total world	19,202.33	7,910.71	11,291.62	100.00	–
Total region	14,241.39	3,508.10	10,733.29	74.16	–
Asia					
Hong Kong	8,416.53	710.41	7,706.12	43.84	1
Japan	3,179.94	2,431.67	748.27	16.56	2
Taiwan	1,053.35	–	1,053.35	5.49	3
Macao	273.42	70.60	202.82	1.42	6
Singapore	140.65	14.72	125.93	0.73	7
South Korea	120.25	–	120.25	0.63	8
Thailand	84.32	–	84.32	0.44	9
Malaysia	24.67	–	24.67	0.13	11
Indonesia	20.17	–	20.17	0.11	12
Philippines	19.02	2.50	16.55	0.10	13
Vietnam	9.02	–	9.02	0.05	14
North Korea	5.94	0.5	5.44	0.03	15
North America	**856.10**	**277.79**	**578.51**	**4.46**	–
United States	581.14	61.70	519.44	3.03	4
Canada	274.96	215.89	59.07	1.43	5
South Pacific	**37.98**	**0.11**	**37.87**	**0.19**	–
Australia	35.16	0.11	35.05	0.18	10
New Zealand	2.82	–	2.82	0.01	16

Source: Adapted from *Statistical Yearbook of China, 1993*, pp. 648–649.

Note: Figures may not add to totals due to rounding.

the Asia Development Bank provided $187.8 million, or 1 percent of the total. Total loans by international organizations to China amounted to $1.3 billion, or 6.8 percent of total foreign capital entering China.

China's economy is tightly integrated into the East Asian economy. Countries within the Asia-Pacific region play varying roles in China's economic development, and relations between China and leading Asian countries differ in characteristics.

Economic Relations with Hong Kong and Taiwan

Mainland China's closest trade and investment relationships are with Hong Kong and Taiwan. In 1992, almost 40 percent of China's total trade was with Hong Kong and Taiwan, which together supplied about half of its foreign investment. Since China opened to foreign investment, Hong Kong has been a dominant trading partner and investor, accounting for 35.1 percent of total trade and 43.8 percent of foreign investment in 1992.

Hong Kong began investing in mainland China as soon as China opened its doors to the world. Initially, the purpose of Hong Kong's investment was to take advantage of the mainland's cheap labor and land, thereby reducing production costs. Since the mid-1980s, because of the success of its early investments in China and the increase in its own domestic labor costs, Hong Kong has invested a large amount in China, especially in Guangdong Province. Hong Kong has shifted a large portion of its manufacturing capacity to the mainland in labor-intensive industries such as clothing, footwear, toys, electronics, textiles, and plastics. Although these industries do not manufacture high-technology products, they have created many job opportunities for China. In the Pearl River delta alone, Hong Kong manufacturing employs more than 3 million workers.

In 1992, when China began to open its domestic market, Hong Kong's investment in China also shifted away from labor-intensive industries toward marketing and infrastructure projects. Huge investments are put to use in the construction of seaports, airports, highways, power stations, industrial parks, and real estate throughout the country.

China has also invested much capital in Hong Kong. According to estimates by the Hong Kong and Shanghai Banking Corporation in Hong Kong, China had invested about $12 billion in Hong Kong by the first quarter of 1992. In fact, China is Hong Kong's most important foreign investor, illustrating the deep integration of the two economies.

Taiwan was mainland China's fourth largest trading partner in 1992. From $320 million in 1980, Taiwan's trade with the mainland increased to $4.2 billion in 1991, growing at an average rate of 26.5 percent annually; it jumped to $6.58 billion in 1992, 55.4 percent over 1991. Taiwan was also mainland China's third largest investor in 1991 and 1992, behind Hong Kong and Japan.

Taiwan's total foreign investment in the mainland grew 120 percent in 1992 for an overall share of 5.55 percent.

Taiwan's investment in mainland China began in 1983 with small-scale projects concentrated in the coastal area of southern China. In 1986, the publication of "Priorities for Promoting Taiwan Business Investing in mainland Economic Zones" strongly stimulated investment to the mainland from Taiwan. In November1992, the Ministry of Economics in Taiwan permitted mainland investment projects of less than $1 million without going through a third party, further stimulating Taiwan's investment in the mainland. By the end of 1993, a total of about $17 billion in contracted investment, or about $5 billion in actual investment, had come from Taiwan.

Although Taiwan's investment in the mainland has been spread throughout the country, it is concentrated in Fujian and Guangdong provinces, each of which takes about one-third of Taiwan's total investment. The scale of Taiwan's investment is considered small, around $1 million a project. Larger projects from Taiwan have only recently come to the mainland, with one project involving more than $100 million. Unlike investment from other sources, investment from Taiwan is usually fully owned by Taiwan's businessmen. Wholly owned firms represent 56.5 percent of total investment, and joint ventures constitute 43.5 percent of the total. Taiwan-based investment has moved in recent years to high-technology, high-value-added industries of machinery, electronics, electric cables, and chemicals. This is a change from Taiwan's concentration on labor-intensive industries during the 1980s. Other sectors, such as real estate and services, have also attracted Taiwan investors.

Because Taiwan has no direct trade with the mainland, goods must be transferred through Hong Kong. Consequently, all three parties benefit from the system of receiving orders in Taiwan, manufacturing the goods on the mainland, and transferring them through Hong Kong for export to the world.

What does the future hold for this three-way cooperation? Although Hong Kong will be returned to China in 1997, it will be relatively independent as a Special Administrative Region, especially with regard to economic issues. Therefore, three-party cooperation must continue to be discussed, and several factors could encourage all three to move closer together economically.

First, the economies of mainland China, Hong Kong, and Taiwan are strongly complementary. The mainland possesses the cheap labor, broad markets, and strong research and development bases that Taiwan and Hong Kong need. Taiwan and Hong Kong have the venture capital, management experience, and global marketing network that the mainland requires. The mainland is still competitive in the labor-intensive industries that Taiwan and Hong Kong are vacating. The mainland can provide markets in which Taiwan and Hong Kong can develop high-technology, high-value-added industries such as computers, passenger cars, petrochemicals, and machine tools—industries that lack the larger market and base to develop in Taiwan and Hong Kong.

Second, the disparate economic systems of the mainland, Hong Kong, and Taiwan will grow more similar as the mainland further develops its market economy. This will promote three-party cooperation because trade will become more efficient among broadly similar systems.

Third, the three parties face similar challenges from regional and global economic blocs, and all three share Chinese language, culture, and ethnicity.

Although it is difficult to discuss the unification of the mainland and Taiwan, economic relations among all three parties are clearly becoming closer. Each has its own economic goals, yet none can think only of its own affairs without considering the impact on others. Economic integration is now emerging. True integration in the largest sense requires both an institutional arrangement to permit transfer of the factors of production among cooperative members *and* coordinated macroeconomic and industrial policies. Currently, this is not foreseeable. Still, coordination and cooperation among the three parties, and movement toward their economic integration, will be unavoidable.

Because economic relations between the mainland and Taiwan will certainly progress, their political difficulties will decrease in the future. There will always be bumps, however, and sometimes an accident such as the Thousand Island Lake issue may cause problems for cross-strait normalization. But such incidents are unlikely to affect the basic interests of those concerned. Although there is no timetable for unification, internal demand within China for cooperation realized through common economic interests among the three parties and external pressure in the form of threats from regional and global blocs will be two driving forces for the mainland and Taiwan to come together. These pressures, if strong, may shorten the time required for unification.

Economic Relations with Southeast Asia

China has had historic economic ties with the Southeast Asian countries of Singapore, Indonesia, Malaysia, Thailand, the Philippines, Vietnam, and Cambodia. Their geographic proximity and concentrations of overseas Chinese have made them traditional markets for Chinese products. In addition, economic relations with them have improved recently owing to better political relations. Despite recent rapid increases in trade and investment, however, the degree of economic interaction between China and Southeast Asia remains small relative to China's total. This is because China's endowments are similar to those of these countries: they, as well as China, are rich in labor and natural resources but lack technology, capital, skilled labor, and managerial experience.

In 1992, trade between China and Singapore, Indonesia, Malaysia, and Thailand amounted to about $8.86 billion, or 5.3 percent of China's total trade. Investment from these countries in China was only 1.4 percent of China's total, about $288.8 million in 1992. The rapidity with which Southeast Asia's investment in China has increased, however, has made it China's fastest growing investor group. Total investment in China in 1992, in comparison with 1991 figures, grew 8 times for Indonesia, 2.2 times for the Philippines, 3.3 times for Thailand, 11.3 times for Malaysia, and 1.1 times for Singapore (see table 6.2).

China will continue to promote good relations with the countries of Southeast Asia. However, several problems may delay China in broadening economic relations with Southeast Asia. Some Southeast Asian countries still harbor political misgivings about China and view it as a "potential threat"; the islands in the South China Sea continue to present a problem between China and several other countries. Japan, the United States, and the EU pay great attention to Southeast Asia as an important market and investment site, and China's relations with Southeast Asia will be challenged by these developed countries. Economic relations between Southeast Asia and China are not as strong as those between Southeast Asia and the more advanced countries because of China's limited economic strength. Finally, because of similar economic conditions and industrial structures in China and Southeast Asia, Chinese products are usually similar to those produced by Southeast Asian countries; in a sense, Southeast Asian countries and China compete more than they complement each other.

What can China do to vigorously promote good economic relations with Southeast Asia? First, it can develop multilateral cooperation on different fronts by participating in dialogue with government officials, academics, businessmen, and others to promote mutual understanding. Second, China can cooperate with a variety of countries: more advanced developing countries may need more technological cooperation; some less developed countries need more trade and investment. Third, China can participate in cross-border projects such as the Lanchang River-Mekong River development program, which involves China, Laos, Thailand, Cambodia, and Vietnam, and the Asian road network project involving China, Laos, Thailand, and Myanmar.

Economic Relations among China, the United States, and Japan

China's relations with the two leading economic powers, the United States and Japan, are in many ways its most important. In 1991 and 1992, Japan was China's second largest trading partner and foreign investor, just behind Hong Kong, and China was Japan's second largest trading partner. The United States was China's third largest trading partner and the fourth largest investor, while China was the ninth largest trading partner of the United States.

In terms of advanced technologies and equipment, the United States and Japan are especially significant for Chinese modernization. A large country with diversified industries, China needs not only capital but also cutting-edge technologies that cannot be acquired elsewhere in the region. Japan and the United States have always supplied much equipment to China, which has imported high-technology products such as automobiles, electronic components, communications equipment, aircraft, precision machine tools, precision instruments, and steel.

Japan

Economic relations between China and Japan have improved and increased. In 1993, total trade between China and Japan reached $38 billion, and Japan's trade with China exceeded Hong Kong's to make Japan China's largest trading partner. China also became Japan's second largest trading partner just behind the United States, jumping from fifth place the previous year.

Dramatic changes in Japan promoted China-Japan trade. First, Japan's investment in China accelerated trade. Before 1990, Japan focused mainly on Southeast Asia; China was not central to Japanese investment plans. As the business environment in China has improved during the 1990s, Japan's investment in China has increased. Japan's investment in 1992 was 67.9 percent greater than in 1991 and is beginning to extend inland from Dalian, Shanghai, Tianjin, and Beijing to Wuhan, Chongqing, and Xian. Moreover, Japanese are now investing in high-technology industries as well as labor-intensive ones.

Second, the recession in Japan has provided market opportunities for Chinese products. As Japanese income and purchasing power decrease, cheaper Chinese products attract more cost-conscious Japanese consumers.

Pressured by Western countries and General Agreement on Tariffs and Trade (GATT) requirements, Japan has reduced tariffs on imported agricultural products. Lower tariffs combined with China's geographic advantages has stimulated the export to Japan of Chinese agricultural products, especially frozen foods such as chicken, vegetables, and fish. China's market share of agricultural products sold in Japan has expanded from 17 percent to 35 percent; its market share for garlic has reached 97 percent.

There are some problems, however, in China-Japan trade—the most severe being China's trade deficit with Japan, which has increased along with total trade. In 1992, the trade deficit was $1.98 billion, but it increased by $4.2 billion in the first eight months of 1993.

Another problem is that China's strategy of low pricing is facing challenges from exporters in Southeast Asia and Europe. For example, Italian garment manufacturers are now shipping high-quality, low-priced mens' suits to Japan; competition like this will cause China to lose its market in Japan. A third problem is that China's cheap exports to Japan have threatened some Japanese industries; for example, an influx of Chinese textile products has caused more than 700 factories in Japan to shut down. Trade frictions between the two countries are likely to increase, and Japan is expected to initiate antidumping measures against cheap Chinese products.

The Chinese and Japanese economies are primarily complementary and not directly competitive, a relationship unlikely to change soon. Establishing and maintaining a cooperative economic relationship will therefore benefit both economies.

Because market share is an important consideration for developed countries, China, with its huge potential domestic market, is attractive to Japanese business. China, of course, is also interested in the Japanese market. Common economic interests will tie the two countries together.

United States

The United States is important to China for trade, investment, technology transfer, and training. Since 1979, the United States has been China's third largest trading partner. The U.S. market is more important to China than official Chinese statistics imply. For example, Chinese export statistics exclude entrepôt trade. Some sources estimate that two-thirds of Chinese goods exported to Hong Kong are reexported to the United States, making the U.S. market the single largest one for Chinese goods.[13] In recent years, because of Taiwan's investment in mainland Chinese enterprises, a portion of total exports to Taiwan are also reexported to the U.S. market. According to U.S. figures for 1993, China was the fourth largest source for U.S. imports, the thirteenth largest recipient of U.S. exports, and, overall, the United States' seventh largest trading partner (it was ranked twenty-fourth in 1980).[14]

The U.S. market is a principal reason why the total of mainland Chinese foreign trade exceeded Taiwan's in 1992. According to the *World Journal*, during the first eight months of 1993, total Taiwanese exports to the United States were $16.16 billion and mainland Chinese exports were $15.82 billion—almost equal. A decade earlier, however, in 1983, Taiwan's exports to the United States were twice as high as those of mainland China. Even as late as 1991, Taiwan's exports to the United States were 1.2 times higher than the mainland's. This shift reflects the Mainland's growing competitiveness in industries once strong in Taiwan.

Investment is important to China-U.S. economic relations. By early 1994, U.S. companies had more than 12,000 projects in China with cumulative contracted investment of $14.4 billion and actual utilized investment of $8.4 billion. In 1993, breaking previous records for U.S. investment in China, U.S. companies invested in 6,750 projects, with contract value capital of $7.3 billion; actual utilized capital was $2.66 billion. In 1994, the United States was now the second largest investor in China. Of the 500 largest U.S. companies, 52—including IBM, Motorola, Procter &

Gamble, General Electric, Dupont, and Xerox—have invested in China; their total contracted investment is $3.66 billion, half the total U.S. investment in China.

Investment by multinational corporations (MNCs) is a milestone for China. MNCs focus on the long term, can bear larger risks than small firms, and usually earmark a significant portion of their profits for reinvestment. The presence of MNCs can help to reinforce a nation's political stability and influence development policies by improving infrastructural conditions, conserving natural resources, promoting high labor standards, and increasing the size of the domestic consumer market. U.S.-based MNCs have found that China's conditions are now favorable for foreign investment. Their presence in China will have a strong positive influence on midsize and small foreign businesses interested in coming to China.

China wishes to accelerate its GNP growth and open further to the world to acquire additional advanced technologies so it can improve the living standards of its citizens and modernize. Most imported technologies in China are from the United States; the United States has been the single largest technology supplier to China since the early 1970s. From 1973 to 1988, China imported 745 sets of equipment and technology from the United States worth $3.4 billion, which represented 21.3 percent of China's total expenditure on imported technologies. In 1990, the contracted value of technologies imported from the United States was $320 million, or 25.2 percent of the total value. Germany ranked a distant second with $114 million at 8.96 percent of total value.[15] Chinese spending on U.S. technology has held steady at about one-quarter of all Chinese expenditures on imported technology.

Technology transfer has always been one of the sensitive issues in China-U.S. relations. Owing to unsteady bilateral political relations and problems concerning intellectual property rights, technology transfer from the United States to China during the last decade has not been stable and smooth. It will remain a contentious issue for both countries in the near future.

Chinese students have been educated and trained in the United States in a variety of fields. Many of them have returned to China to make great contributions to China's economic development. Although difficult to measure, this benefit to China is nevertheless notable.

Strategic Uncertainty and Implications for China's Economic Relations

In the 1990s, the most important economic issues between the United States and China are most-favored-nation (MFN) trade status, the U.S. trade deficit with China, and intellectual property rights. The MFN issue was resolved by President Bill Clinton in May 1994, when he announced that the United States would no longer link human rights issues with MFN trade status for China. China can be expected to pay more attention to some aspects of human rights.

Although the trade deficit is an issue between the two countries, it should not prove intolerable to the United States because concepts differ between the two sides. Finally, rifts created between China and the United States over intellectual property rights are not irreparable. China has realized that insufficient protection of these rights would hurt Chinese as well as foreign business. In fact, as a developing country starting at a very poor level economically, China has done as much as possible since the late 1980s on the issue of intellectual property rights. Laws and government regulations have been created and implemented. The overall outlook for China-U.S. economic relations is not pessimistic.

A broader look at the triangular relationship among the United States, Japan, and China does not present as pleasant a picture. Although each country receives benefits from the others, each also has concerns about the others. China worries about rising militarism in Japan and about the ideological threat, political pressure, and economic sanctions of the United States. Japan worries about China's growing economic and military strength and about trade disagreements with the United States.

In the post-cold war period the United States occupies a difficult foreign policy position because it cannot identify who will become an enemy and where strategic threats will arise. Japan, as a longtime U.S. ally, is not only taking over the U.S. economic position in the Asia-Pacific region but also threatening the U.S. economy in the North American market. Because of uncertain elements in Russia and the difficulty of predicting its strategic direction, the United States must retain a strategic capability toward that country. A fast-growing Chinese economy means both opportunity and challenge to the United States. On the one hand, the United States does not want to lose China's market to quibbling over ideology; on the other hand, it does not want a too-strong China in the Asia-Pacific region.

The distrust among China, Japan, and the United States keeps any two of them from allying to fight against the third. The United States, as the leading power during the cold war, has remained the power able to preserve order in the Asia-Pacific but of course worries that any rising or falling regional power could upset the balance and threaten existing U.S. interests in the region. Because both Japan and China are in the category of rising powers, U.S. decision making may be difficult.

U.S. political and strategic uncertainty affects U.S. foreign economic relations and causes many of the frictions and bumps in its economic relations with Japan and with China. A series of examples makes this clear: Since early 1994, the U.S. trade representative has criticized 44 countries for unfair trade practices and has tried to apply sanctions under its Super 301 act. Japan was the first target, followed by the EU and China. In June 1994, the United States set quantitative indicators to measure the access to the Japanese market of U.S. goods. China was bothered by the MFN issue until May 1994. Trade relations have never been so contentious. This is a reflection of the uncertain direction of foreign policies and a contradictory mentality.

Uncertainty in U.S.-Asia policy and strategy also affects U.S. economic relations with countries such as South Korea and members of the Association of Southeast Asian Nations (ASEAN) and has caused trade frictions with them. The certainty of U.S. foreign policy is one of the core elements for economic stability and the development of East Asia.

In sum, China's economic development has been tightly linked to the world market, especially to the Asia-Pacific region, since the early 1980s. Although all economies in this region play an important role in China's development, Hong Kong, Japan, Taiwan, and the United States are China's major partners in trade and investment. These four comprise 65 percent of trade shares and 70 percent of investment shares in China and are the main financial sources for China.

A dynamic Chinese economy also benefits from regional economies. In a purely economic sense, the future for economic development of each member and for cooperation among members is bright. Unfortunately, an inharmonious tone unfavorable for Chinese economic development sometimes is heard, expressed as "China will be a threat to rest of the world" and "China will fill the power vacuum in Asia." Actually, the lack of confidence among world leaders is the key reason for economic discord in this region.

China's Role in Regional Development

Two of today's key global issues are peace and development. With one-fifth of the world's people, China has the world's largest population. If it cannot develop and remains poor, it would be a burden not only for itself but for the world; but a developed China could make a major contribution to the world.

Many believe that the next century will be the Pacific century. But the only developed countries in the Asia-Pacific region are the United States, Canada, Japan, Australia, New Zealand, and the Four Dragons—Singapore, Hong Kong, South Korea, and Taiwan. Their combined population is about 500 million. China's population is one-third of Asia's total population of 3 billion. Without China as one of the developed countries, how can there be talk of a Pacific century?

The development of China's economy and improvement in its economic strength provide other Asia-Pacific economies with many opportunities and markets for trade and investment. China's total foreign trade is forecast to reach $400 billion by the end of this century. From 1994 to the year 2000, the gross value of Chinese imports will be about $1,000 billion. The great size of the Chinese market is clear, as is its potential importance to countries of the region.

Since China's economy opened to the world, it has been tightly linked to the world economy, especially the Asia-Pacific economy. Now, after 15 years of development, the Chinese economy has entered a new period that requires a new economic structure consisting of agriculture, manufacturing, and tertiary industry or services. Any changes in Chinese agriculture, manufacturing, or other major industries will in turn affect the economic and financial development of the Asia-Pacific region.

China's economic development is severely restricted by its lack of modern agricultural methods. Shortages of rice, wheat, vegetable oil, and cotton would likely cause social instability. Poor weather, pests, or other causes of lower agricultural output would force China to increase its imports of agricultural products. Guangdong Province, for example, has had to increase its imports of rice from Thailand, and other developed areas such as Hainan and Fujian soon will follow Guangdong's path.

In manufacturing, many enterprises need to update their products, equipment, and technologies; and most will depend on imports. For example, China imported 59,600 sets of machine tools in 1991. It expects to spend $350 billion to $400 billion on foreign imports, mainly equipment and technology, during the Eighth Five-Year Plan (1990–1995). This trend will continue and will certainly affect the market in the Asia-Pacific.

Tertiary industry—especially real estate, telecommunications, and finance—has been a booming sector in China in recent years and provides many opportunities for foreign investors. These industries have become the hottest fields for foreign companies.

Regional and subregional cooperation is a growing phenomenon. Four areas of subregional cooperation surround China: the South China Sea cooperation area, including Hong Kong, Taiwan, Guangdong, Fujian, and Hainan; the East China Sea cooperation area, including Taiwan, Hong Kong, Japan, Shanghai, Jiangsu, Zhejiang, and Shandong; the Northeast Asia cooperation area, including Liaoning, Jilin, Heilongjiang, South Korea, North Korea, Japan, and Russia; and the Mekong River cooperation area, including Guangxi, Yunnan, Guizhou, Vietnam, Thailand, Laos, and Myanmar. These subregions have developed closer relations with one another and, with China as their center, are playing a greater role in the Asia-Pacific.

The invitation to China to attend the Asia-Pacific Economic Cooperation (APEC) meeting in Seattle in 1993 illustrated China's role in regional cooperation. After Dr. Mahathir Mohamad, prime minister of Malaysia, proposed an independent East Asian Economic Caucus (EAEC) in 1990, Chinese Premier Li Peng added his support during a visit to Malaysia in 1994. Although China usually agrees to support any type of inclusive regional cooperation, its support boosted Dr. Mahathir's proposal to create an independent organization sans U.S. participation.

Although it is a strong force in the Asia-Pacific, China does not demand to be a leader in the region or to create a regional cooperative group with itself as the center. But it must be involved with organizations for regional cooperation.

China's Foreign Policy in the Context of Development

As mentioned above, two of today's key global issues are peace and development. Because China calculated in the late 1970s that a future world war would not be possible, it discontinued its political struggle and immediately began economic construction. China has since altered its industrial structure to facilitate economic development. Beginning in the late 1970s, for example, China converted much of its military production to civilian use, thereby avoiding the suffering of many countries that began reducing their military production only in the late 1980s. China has completed its defense conversion while other countries are still bearing the burden of military production.

Because China's central task is economic construction, it requires a peaceful and stable international environment and needs to maintain friendly relations with all neighbors. Therefore, China must conduct a peaceful foreign policy, especially one through which it vows never to seek a superpower or leadership role in the world. This policy, which Deng Xiaoping has stated is China's policy for today as well as for the future—even after China is developed—should relieve China's neighbors. They should find no reason to prepare for contingencies vis-à-vis China.

No policy, however good, will be able to solve all the problems created by China's fast-growing economy. Negative economic contingencies still exist and include four issues: inflation, the economic disparity between China's coast and its interior, relations with Taiwan, and the dispute in the South China Sea.

A high growth rate without inflation is ideal. Almost all high growth, however, will be accompanied by severe inflation. China has had three periods of inflation since it began its economic reform: the first was in 1985 with a 9.4 percent rate of inflation; the second, 1988 with an average inflation rate of 11.9 percent; and the third, December 1993, when inflation reached its highest rate, 26.7 percent. In 1994, inflation averaged 25 percent. Inflation at such a high rate over a period as long as two years could be dangerous to China and cause severe problems, especially social instability.

Some in China disregard inflation and believe rapid economic growth and development are sustainable. In fact, there is no positive correlation between inflation and economic development; economic development does not need to be supported by inflation.

Inflation hurts many groups of people, especially low-income workers. China's political turmoil in 1989 was caused, at least in part, by the high inflation of 1988. Professors and students, in low-income and no-income groups, were hurt by high inflation and made their complaints known to the government. Today the situation for most professors has improved. Students, however, still belong to a no-income group and are still active. China should always pay attention to the inflation rate and should keep the maintenance of social stability its central task.

The economic disparity between the coast and the interior is another potentially dangerous problem for China if there is no way to narrow regional differences. Unfortunately, the disparities have increased since China began economic reform.

Taiwan will be another sensitive issue for the mainland. Taiwan's independence movement has been strong of late; in addition to this problem, there has been pressure to internationalize and thereby complicate the unification issue. That some countries choose to support Taiwan makes the situation even more complex. Yet the mainland has never renounced the use of force to maintain a unified China; therefore there might be a danger if Taiwan acted to become independent.

China has good relations with almost all its neighbors. The South China Sea is China's only source of dispute with some countries. About 43 coral islands in the South China Sea are occupied by other countries, 6 islands are controlled by mainland China, and one island is controlled by Taiwan. Although China has suggested that interested countries develop the area together and solve the dispute later on—a proposition agreed to by Vietnam and ASEAN—countries in the region remain poised to contend with China over natural resources in the South China Sea.

How can the risk inherent in these issues be reduced? China believes that, rather than using force, the best way is by improving its own economic strength and extending economic cooperation to these countries. China would like to negotiate with these governments individually and not internationalize the issue. Bilateral rather than multilateral negotiations would make these issues easier to resolve.

Some observers have implied that China threatens other countries when it renews its military strength and improves its economic position. This conclusion is not the only one that may be reached when considering the facts of the regional and global situation. Clearly, however, China will not give up its basic national interests, territory, and sovereignty.

7

The Future of China's Economy

China's economic development is now greatly influenced by the world economy. What is the present condition of the world economy? What are China's challenges, and where do they originate? What is the relationship between China and major countries in East Asia? Where do China's opportunities lie? The answers to these questions have important implications for China's economic development as well as the economic development of East Asia.

The World Economy in the Mid-1990s

In the early 1990s, most Western countries were in economic recession. In 1993, the global economy grew only 2.3 percent.[16] Although no single developed country was a locomotive to pull the world's economic train, the economies of the United States, the UK, and Canada have begun to move out of recession. Western countries still have many problems, however, including high government debt and high unemployment.

Economic growth in the EU has been very slow. Its economy stagnated in 1993; unemployment reached 11 percent, or 16 million. The main reason for European economic problems was the slowdown of the German economy. After the two Germanies unified, eastern Germany absorbed huge amounts of capital. To support eastern Germany, Germany increased its budget in 1992 to 180 billion marks from 140 billion marks the year before, an amount equaling 5 percent of Germany's GNP. About three-quarters of the total increase was spent on public consumption and social expenses, not on investment in production. The results were no profits, a capital account deficit, high unemployment, and inflation. Through the exchange rate links, Germany's problems pulled down the entire European economy.

Japan is in its worst economic position since the end of World War II. The bubble economy burst, reducing domestic market demand; a cool summer in 1993 caused a shortfall in the output of rice; and a high trade surplus caused a rapid appreciation of the Japanese yen. Europe and Japan are still dealing with the effects of recession, and their attention will remain on readjusting their economic policies to solve their domestic economic problems.

The economies of Russia, other countries of the Commonwealth of Independent States, and Eastern Europe remain troubled. In 1993, Russia's economy shrank by about 15 percent and inflation reached 1,000 percent. Russia's economic difficulties severely hurt its standard of living. About 35 percent of Russians earn only $25 per month, making it difficult for them to meet the basic needs of life. Other countries in the CIS have experienced economic troubles because of unstable domestic politics, inappropriate economic policies, and lack of economic aid from Western countries.

The economies of Poland, Hungary, and the Czech Republic have started to grow. Poland's GNP growth rate reached 2 percent in 1993, making it the best performing economy in Eastern Europe. Because the former Yugoslavia is still involved in a civil war, it is not possible to predict economic improvements there.

In Latin America, the last decade was a lost decade; except for Brazil, Mexico, and Argentina, no economies improved significantly. In Africa, the past decade was marked by the misery of disaster, famine, and war. Both southern continents have a certain distance to travel before they can begin normal economic development.

East Asia is a unique region, characterized by political stability and vibrant economic development. According to International Monetary Fund statistics, the average GDP growth rate in Western countries in 1992 was about 1.8 percent, but growth in Asian countries averaged 7.8 percent (see table 7.1). The Four Dragons and the ASEAN countries have developed rapidly since the 1960s. Average annual growth of the Four Dragons was 9.3 percent in the 1960s, 9.2 percent in the 1970s, and 7.9 percent in the 1980s. The average growth rate in the ASEAN countries, excluding Singapore, was 6 percent in the 1960s, 7.3 percent in the 1970s, and 5.8 percent in the 1980s.

China's growth rate in the 1980s averaged 9 percent per year and allowed it to join the group of fast-growing Asian countries. After 30 years of continuous economic growth, East Asia's share of global economic output increased to 27 percent in 1990, up from only 4 percent in 1960, and will reach one-third of world

Table 7.1
GDP Growth: G-7 Countries and Select Asian Countries, 1989–1992
(in percentages)

	1989	1990	1991	1992
G-7 countries	**3.1**	**2.3**	**0.4**	**1.8**
United States	2.5	1.2	-0.7	2.6
Japan	4.7	4.8	4.0	1.3
Germany[a]	3.6	5.7	1.7	1.9
France	4.3	2.5	0.7	1.4
Italy	2.9	2.1	1.3	0.9
Canada	2.4	-0.2	-1.7	0.7
United Kingdom	2.2	0.4	-2.2	-0.5
Select Asian countries				
China	4.2	4.3	7.8	13.0
Hong Kong	2.8	3.2	4.2	5.0
South Korea	6.2	9.2	8.5	4.8
Malaysia	9.2	9.7	8.7	8.0
Singapore	9.2	8.3	6.7	5.8
Taiwan	7.6	4.9	7.2	6.6
Thailand	12.0	10.0	8.2	7.5

Sources: World Economic Outlook, International Monetary Fund, October 1993; Chen Jimin, "The Trend of the World Economic Development," *Foreign Social Sciences* (Nanjing), no. 12 (1993).

[a] Data through 1990 apply to West Germany only.

GNP within a decade. Japan accounts for 16 percent of world GNP while other Asian countries account for 11 percent.[17] East Asia has become the most dynamic region in the world.

East Asia has formed a new growth pole as each country or area has adjusted its industrial structure, reformed its economic system, and established complementary economic relations. Although East Asia has yet to become a formal bloc such as the EU or NAFTA, cooperation exists and East Asia will maintain its dynamic development.

What is the future of the world economy? The United States, with 25 percent of the world GNP, the EU with 25 percent, and Japan with 16 percent have created a multipolar global economic structure. The EU will further integrate in the next several years. To compete with the EU, the United States, Canada, and Mexico have enacted the North American Free Trade Agreement

(NAFTA). Japan, as a traditional leader in East Asia, would like to form and lead a regional cooperative organization to compete with the other two blocs. The global economy will be characterized by increased formal regionalization.

Countries and blocs will compete to develop science and technology to enhance economic strength. With the end of the cold war, the question of leadership of each bloc will be determined by economic strength and technological position. Competition will become increasingly intense.

Competition among both less developed countries and developing countries will sharpen. Because more countries are adopting the market system, their economies have become more vibrant. Russia and East European countries will soon resume economic growth. South Asia and Latin America will also be increasing their competitive strength.

Challenges and Opportunities for China

Facing strong competition, an open China will meet both challenges and opportunities. The most serious challenges are the slowdown of the world economy and the politicization of economic relationships with other states.

The world economic slowdown hurt not only developed countries but also developing countries, including China. Decreases in income and increases in unemployment in developed countries due to the worldwide economic slowdown have limited the market for Chinese products abroad. To maintain its target export growth rate, China has had to either reduce export prices or shift its mix of exported products. The global economic downturn has hurt China's export growth.

Many countries are politicizing economic relations or attempting to achieve their political goals through economic means. After the cold war, countries paid more attention to their economies. Economics became the priority in international relations. The United States has linked political conditions such as human rights and democracy to trade.

The economic recession in advanced countries forced them to restructure their industries to become more competitive. Shifting industrial structures provided opportunities for China to upgrade its own industrial structure. Since the Clinton administration emphasized development of high technologies and encouraged the export of technological products, China has benefited by allowing IBM, Apple, Compaq, and Motorola to enter the Chinese market. These companies are the large, high-technology companies in the fields of computers and telecommunications that China needs. The Chinese computer industry now exports about $1.560 billion worth of computer parts, components, and finished machines to the world, up from almost nothing before 1993, when foreign computer companies arrived in China. Also, the appreciation of the Japanese yen, which has forced Japanese companies to reduce or discontinue domestic production of some products, has been an opportunity for Japan to expand production capacity in China to take advantage of China's lower costs. Japan has had to reduce its production of steel, but China is expanding its production.

China's low land and labor costs, relatively good infrastructure, and large domestic market have attracted many foreign companies searching for business opportunities. China, in turn, receives large amounts of capital, advanced technologies, and management experience. Foreign investment has become important for China as it attempts to deal with capital shortages.

China's Competitive Strategy

China would like to maximize opportunities and minimize challenges in today's fast-changing world. To achieve a fourfold increase in GNP during the last two decades of the twentieth century—the goal of China's national economic development emphasized by Deng Xiaoping—the Chinese government outlined a detailed plan. The government plan must promote a market economic system, create a modern enterprise system, create stability on the "twenty words principle," and engage the world economy.

The market economic system and the modern enterprise system, two strategies approved during the 14th Congress of the CCP in November 1993, support the Chinese economy like two legs support one person. Economic development would be unbalanced and incomplete if China were to pursue only one of these strategies and reject the other. The market economy will transform China's macroeconomic conditions while the modern enterprise system transforms China's microeconomic conditions. The market system improves competitiveness by using market mechanisms to operate the national economy, to allocate natural resources and social resources, and to increase efficiency.

The features of a modern enterprise system should be introduced into China's state-owned enterprise sector. As the foundation of the Chinese national economy, state-owned enterprises play an important role. However, people believe that to suit a market economy, a modern enterprise system must be created. Modern enterprises are characterized by

- clearly defined property rights. State property within a firm belongs to the state, but firms possess personal property rights to enable a legal person to operate a firm and bear its rights and liabilities;

- an independent operation by the firm's own management and workforce who are responsible for losses, gains, and tax obligations;

- investor rights to share in firm benefits and to carry only limited liability if the business goes bankrupt; and

- independent decision making and noninterference by government in daily operations.

The modern enterprise system is the foundation of the market economic system. Introducing a dynamic enterprise system with clear rights and liabilities will stimulate China's state-owned enterprises to increase their efficiency and competitive strength. This will increase their ability to compete in the world market.

The "twenty words principle"—twenty Chinese characters that signify grasping opportunities, deepening reforms, expanding openness, promoting development, and maintaining stability—states concisely Deng Xiaoping's ideas on developing China. Stability is key. Reform, openness, and development cannot be achieved without social and political stability; and social and political stability depend on reform, openness, and development. This is true not only in China but in most of East Asia. The Asian Development Bank summarized these relationships when it reported on the experience of the Four Dragons. In late 1992 and early 1993, China learned the lesson that all of these factors must be balanced to avoid economic overheating. China must balance stability and development. In the Third Plenum of the 14th Congress of the CCP, the "twenty words principle" became an official guide for China's domestic economic construction and international competition.

Believing that autarky will gain nothing for China, China plans to engage more widely with the world economy. China can learn from the other successful newly industrializing economies and strengthen itself for world competition. Already strong after 15 years of openness, China will open its economy even further to engage the world, but not without gaining something— advanced technology or capital investment—in return. China will gain necessities for its domestic economy as foreign companies enter the Chinese domestic market.

Although the Chinese government has never announced a systematic policy on regional cooperation in the Asia-Pacific, some points are clear. First, China has felt the strong pressure of recent trends in globalization and regionalization. Second, the Asia-Pacific region has not created a clear framework for regional cooperation even though the EU and NAFTA are increasingly strong, organized competitors; therefore China must find a position for itself. Third, because of the variety of social, political, and economic systems in the region, China believes regional cooperation should be open, inclusive, more flexible, practical, and varied. It cannot be an exclusive, rigid framework.

Finally, China strongly prefers that regional cooperation not be dominated by any one country—by the United States or Japan, for example. China will not assert its leadership in this region because China believes that members in a cooperative framework should be equals. The United States and Japan, on the basis of their economic strength, are trying to be leaders in Asia-Pacific regional cooperation, and China will not try to stop them. But China will not follow them blindly; it will maintain its independent ideas and actions according to its own interests.

In the future, China will create a system of open economic cooperation, pay more attention to relations with surrounding countries, and participate in various regional cooperative ventures:

- It will readjust its export market structure to reduce its overdependence on the U.S., Japanese, and EU markets, which will in turn reduce trade frictions.

- It will emphasize an improvement of trade relations with Southeast Asia and South America.

- It will promote a new order in the Asia-Pacific because there is great potential in the region. Without a peaceful and stable international environment and fair and reasonable regional relations, the Asia-Pacific will not realize its potential.

Prospects for Economic Development and Reform

Deng Xiaoping's blueprint for Chinese development described three stages: China's GNP should double between 1980 and 1990; its GNP should double again and GNP per capita should reach $1,000 by the end of the year 2000; and its GNP should once again double and per capita GNP reach $4,000 by 2050. If China's population is 1.5 billion in 2050, GNP would reach $6 trillion. China would then join the group of countries in the mid-development stage.

To realize Deng's blueprint, some believe China should grow as fast as it can; some believe China should choose stability over a high growth rate; and some believe the regions of China should move forward each at its own speed because specific regional conditions differ. When people assess the speed of China's economic growth over the last two years, some in China think that the economy has not been overheated and that tighter macroeconomic control is not necessary. Some in academic society and some in the business world, especially in the coastal areas, oppose macroeconomic controls. But the majority disagree, not only because of the problems noted earlier but because of the memories of June 1989, when the overheated economy caused high inflation and social instability. China cannot give up social stability for a high growth rate.

There has been no firm consensus about how to control the economy. The government decided earlier to control only those sectors with serious problems and not tighten the key sectors—energy, telecommunications, and transportation. Solutions for problem sectors will not be found only through administrative means but through economic and legal means as well.

Certain economic problems are ongoing. Economic reform in urban industries has not been ideal. State-owned enterprises still do not function with enough vitality. Problems from China's pre-reform period persist at both the microeconomic and macroeconomic levels. Some problems are becoming more serious—especially the inefficiency of state-owned enterprises, the decline in central government revenue, energy and transportation bottlenecks, and foreign trade frictions. These ongoing problems are forcing China to accelerate its economic reforms.

The biggest burden for the Chinese economy in upcoming years will be the low vitality of state-owned enterprises. China must implement the policies outlined in "The Regulations for Shifting Operational Mechanisms for State-owned Enterprises" to revitalize the money-losing state-owned enterprises. Chinese enterprises must adopt a modern, standard management system to clarify property rights and enhance the competitiveness of state-owned enterprises. The ministry-level State Economic and Trade Commission (SETC) plans to grant operational rights to 10,000 enterprises, to inspect state-owned property at 1,000 key enterprises, and to test modern management systems in about 100 selected enterprises. The SETC has identified 10 cities in which to explore increasing the operating capital for state-owned enterprises to reduce their dependency on bank loans. The government is continuing to test and expand a stockholding system. Social security, housing, and foreign trade also are undergoing reform also.

The government will continue to promote China's engagement with the world economy to develop natural resources and international markets. The Chinese yuan will be a convertible currency in the near future. This reengagement includes China's return to the GATT, now the World Trade Organization.

More trading businesses will open. Command planning will be abolished. Except for a few important goods, products now controlled by the government will be released.

The government is supporting the formation of large comprehensive trading groups. Large production groups will be encouraged to combine with the trading companies to increase competitiveness and efficiency through economies of scale.

Implementing consistent foreign trade policies in all regions and increasing the transparency of China's trade policies are ongoing policy goals. Only published laws, regulations, and policy can be legal, valid, and implemented. Local governments will not have the right to independently create new international trade policies or regulations.

Domestically, China will try to shape a market economic system and, internationally, try to engage with the world market. China's goal is clear: develop economically as fast as possible while enhancing stability as much as possible. This is the model of most East Asian countries and the essence of the development miracle of East Asia.

Conclusion

China has made considerable progress in its reform, which will help further its development. Recent large-scale capital investment could increase China's productivity. Important industries—iron, steel, cement, electricity, seaports, railways, and air transport—are increasing capacity rapidly. Fast-increasing foreign investment has raised not only Chinese productivity but also the level of Chinese technology and competitiveness, thus enhancing the economic environment for further development.

Capital investment, which generated China's earlier rapid economic growth, is still high. Large-scale infrastructure construction requires large amounts of investment, as do agriculture and development in the western part of China.

Economic reform could be advantageous for China. China's turn toward a market economy will no doubt increase the potential of the Chinese economy as efficiency and capacity rise. Yet drawbacks are also apparent. Economic reform requires large amounts of scarce capital to support it. Because it is accelerating enterprise reform, China needs to establish a social security system to support workers affected by bankruptcy. Transforming existing enterprises into high-technology firms also requires capital investment. Because systems are changing rapidly, uncompleted economic operational systems and legal systems will cause high inflation and corruption, problems that may force China to reduce the speed of its development.

The future of Chinese economic development relies on further economic reform. The Chinese economy has not escaped its vicious circle of stop-and-go growth for several reasons: enterprise efficiency remains low, and China is unable to cope with unemployment and the possibility of social instability.

In a broader sense, China's economic development depends on global as well as regional stability and development. And the stability and prosperity of the Asia-Pacific region depend on relations among its members—especially China, Japan, and the United States.

There is a fundamental misunderstanding in the United States about Chinese development—i.e., that a strong China will threaten U.S. interests in the long run. But China is, in fact, only a developing country—albeit the largest one. The goal for developing countries is to catch up with advanced countries to improve the lives of their citizens. This goal requires that developing countries be aggressive economically. China is no exception.

With modernization as its central task, China is sparing no effort to achieve economic development, which may make China appear to be aggressive although it is not. Advanced countries do not always have clear goals either. They are always in a defensive position, trying to retain their primacy and seeming to be in opposition to the developing countries, but this is not necessarily the case. "Catching up" is a natural human trait that causes competition but not necessarily confrontation. Given that premise, the problems among China, the United States, and Japan will be solved, creating a stable and peaceful environment favorable for all parties in the region.

Notes

1.   *Statistical Yearbook of China, 1993* (Beijing: China Statistical Publishing House, 1994), 31.

2.   The Four Modernizations were enunciated in Premier Chou En-lai's report on the work of government at the Fourth National People's Congress, January 1975: "In this century, we must accomplish the all-out modernization of agriculture, industry, national defense, and science and technology, so that our country's national economy proceeds into the front row of the world!"

3.   State Statistical Bureau, "The Statistic Report on 1993's National Economy and Social Development," *China Statistic*, no. 3 (1994): 7–11. Liu Guoguang et al., "China in 1994: Economic Analysis and Forecast" (Beijing: China Social Sciences Press, 1993), 5–6, 38–39.

4.   *International Business*, July 29, 1993; *Economic Daily* (Beijing), February 1, 1994.

5.   All dollar amounts, unless stated otherwise, are U.S. dollars. The majority of statistical information is based on Chinese sources, however. In 1980 the exchange rate was U.S.$1 = 1.7 yuan; at the end of 1992, U.S.$1 = 5.5 yuan; at the end of 1993, U.S.$1 = 8.7 yuan; and in April 1995, U.S.$1 = 8.3 yuan.

6.   *Coastal areas*, which include the municipalities of Beijing, Tianjin, and Shanghai and the provinces of Liaoning, Hebei, Shandong, Jiangsu, Zhejiang, Fujian, Guangdong, Guangxi, and Hainan, account for 13.8 percent of China's total territory and 41.25 percent of the total population (using 1990 figures).

The interior includes China's central and western regions. *Central China* includes the provinces of Heilongjiang, Jilin, Inner Mongolia, Shanxi, Henan, Hubei, Hunan, Anhui, and Jiangxi and comprises 29.8 percent of total territory and 35.68 percent of the total population. *China's western provinces and autonomous regions*—Shaanxi, Ningxia, Gangsu, Xinjiang, Sichuan, Yunnan, Guizhou, and Tibet—encompass 56.4 percent of total territory and 23.07 percent of the total population.

7.   Wei Houkai and Liu Kai, "Analysis and Forecast on China's Regional Differences and Trends," *China Industrial Economics Research* (Beijing), no. 3 (1994): 29–30.

8.   State Committee for Economic Structure Reform, *China's Economic Structure Reform* no. 8, 1993, pp. 21–23.

9. *Economic Daily,* March 25, 1994, p. 2.

10. See Li Guoqing, "The Moon of Foreign Investment is Round?" *Economic Management* (Beijing), no. 7 (1994): 55.

11. Ibid.

12. *Statistical Yearbook of China, 1993,* p. 31 and p. 633.

13. Nicholas Lardy, "China's Growing Economic Role in Asia," *Analysis* (National Bureau of Asian Research, Seattle, Washington) 3, no. 3 (1992): 3.

14. Zhou Shijian, "Development is the Principal Trend of Sino-U.S. Economic and Trade Relations," *Newspaper of Economic Reference* (Beijing), September 9, 1994, p. 3.

15. *Almanac of China's Economy* (Beijing: Economic Management Press, 1991), iii–214.

16. International Monetary Fund, *World Economic Output* (October 1994).

17. Chen Jimin, "The Trend of World Economic Development," *Foreign Social Sciences* (Nanjing), no. 12 (1993).

About the Editors

A Rhodes scholar with M.Phil. and Ph.D. degrees in international relations from Oxford, GERRIT W. GONG holds the Freeman Chair in China Studies at CSIS and has directed the CSIS Asian Studies Program since 1989. Dr. Gong's government experience includes service in the U.S. State Department as Special Assistant to Under Secretary of State for Political Affairs Michael H. Armacost and Special Assistant to U.S. Ambassadors Winston Lord and James Lilley at the U.S. Embassy in Beijing. He was a fellow in Sino-Soviet Studies at CSIS from 1981 to 1985. He has also served on the faculties of The Johns Hopkins University School of Advanced International Studies and Oxford University. He is author of *The Standard of "Civilization" in International Society* (Clarendon Press, 1984) and has published articles in foreign policy journals in both the United States and Asia, including "A Cross-Strait Summit? Some Observations from Washington," in the January 16, 1995, issue of the *China Times* in Taipei; *The Southeast Asian Boom* with Keith W. Eirinberg; "Defining a New Consensus for U.S. China Policy," in *U.S. China Policy: Building a New Consensus*; and "China's Fourth Revolution," *The Washington Quarterly*, Winter 1994. In May 1994, in testimony before the U.S. Senate Subcommittee on East Asian and Pacific Affairs, Dr. Gong presented "Defining a New Consensus for U.S. China Policy."

As vice president and director of studies at CSIS, ERIK R. PETERSON oversees the development and execution of the Center's broad-based research agenda. He also directs the CSIS publications program, which includes the *Washington Papers* and *Significant Issues* series, and serves as cochairman of the Board of Editors of the Center's quarterly journal, *The Washington Quarterly*. Peterson came to the Center from Kissinger Associates, where he was director of research and head of the firm's Washington, D.C. office. Among his writings are "Looming Collision of Capitalisms?", *The Washington Quarterly,* Spring 1994 and reprinted in Eugene R. Wittkopf (ed.), *The Global Edition* (New York: McGraw-Hill, 1994); "An Agenda for Managing Relations with Russia" and "The Enterprise for the Americas Initiative and a U.S.-Chilean FTA," in Robert E. Hunter and Erik R. Peterson (eds.), *Agenda '93: CSIS Policy Action Papers*, December 1993; *The Gulf Cooperation Council: Search for Unity in a Dynamic Region* (1988); and "The Outlook for the GCC in the Postwar Gulf" in J. E. Peterson, ed., *Saudi Arabia and the Gulf States* (1989). Peterson holds an M.B.A. in finance and international business from the Wharton School of the University of Pennsylvania (1991). He received an M.A. in international law and economics from the Paul H. Nitze School of Advanced International Studies at The Johns Hopkins University and a B.A. in international affairs from Colby College. He also holds the Certificate of Eastern European Studies from the University of Fribourg in Switzerland.

East Asia Economic and Financial Outlook

Other Books in the Series

Taiwan's Economic Role in East Asia
Chi Schive

Chi Schive analyzes Taiwan's rapid development and economic dynamism of the past three decades and looks at the prospects ahead. The author pays particular attention to Taiwan's economic restructuring, its cross-strait trade and investment with the People's Republic of China, and its potential to function as a regional operations center. He also foresees growing competition in the region, which may be the catalyst for continued reforms and upgrading, making the Asia Pacific region a praiseworthy model of "open regionalism."

Contents:

1. Introduction

2. The New Order in East Asia

3. Taiwan's Great Transition in the 1980s

4. Taiwan's Economic Restructuring and Regional Integration

5. Relations between the Two Sides across the Taiwan Strait

6. Taiwan as a Regional Operations Center

7. Taiwan's Role in the Asia-Pacific Region

8. Conclusion

Chi Schive is vice chairman of the Council for Economic Planning and Development of the Executive Yuan in Taipei and, concurrently, professor, chairman, and director of the department of economics, National Taiwan University, Taipei.

Significant Issues Series 1995
ISBN 0-89206-319-X $14.95

Hong Kong's Economic and Financial Future
Y. F. Luk

This volume in the East Asia Economic and Financial Outlook series assesses Hong Kong's phenomenal economic performance of the last few decades and, in particular, its special relationship with the People's Republic of China. The author also examines the changing domestic economic policies and political institutions that have played crucial roles in Hong Kong's growth and asks whether this spectacular growth will continue into the next decade.

Contents:

1. The Hong Kong Economy: Early Development and Salient Features

2. Recent Developments

3. The Outlook for the Hong Kong Economy

4. Conclusion

Y. F. Luk is a lecturer in the School of Economics and Finance at the University of Hong Kong and editor at the Hong Kong Centre for Economic Research.

Significant Issues Series   1995
ISBN 0-89206-306-8 $14.95

❖   ❖   ❖

For information on these and other CSIS publications, contact:

CSISBOOKS
1800 K Street, N.W.
Washington, D.C.   20006
Telephone   202-775-3119
Facsimile   202-775-3199